Introducing Public Administration
Made Simple for TOEIC

최 창 현

도서출판 대영문화사

PREFACE

졸업자는 많고 취업은 어려운 현실이다. 전 세계에서 직업을 구하는 것도 한 방안이다. 영어는 비단 학문을 하기 위한 도구이기도 하지만 전 세계를 무대로 활동하기 위한 도구이기도 하다. 필자의 경우 대학에서 영어원서로 공부할 기회는 행정학개론 원서강독 한 과목뿐이라 정외과에서 개설한 국제정치론, 사회학과의 사회변동론, 산업심리학과의 동기이론, 그리고 영문과의 20세기 영미소설, 18세기 영미소설 등 6과목의 원서로 수업하는 과목을 수강하였다. 이는 내 인생에 아주 중요한 밑거름이 되었다.

또 하나 내 인생에 아주 중요한 밑거름이 된 계기는 1973년 봄의 일로 기억된다. 당시 종로 2가에 위치한 EMI 영어학원에서 새벽 단과반을 수강했었다. 나는 중2였고 수강생들은 대부분 마지막 입시를 목전에 둔 중 3이었다. 교재는 안현필 영어 실력 기초였던 걸로 기억된다.

첫 날 가 보니 한 150여 명 들어가는 강의실에 뒤는 자리가 없고 한 명의 여학생만 있는 앞자리만 한두 줄 비어 있어 선생님이 앞으로 오라고 하셨다. 처음에는 왜 앞줄이 비어 있는지 몰랐다. 매 수업시간 암기할 문장이 한 20여 개 적혀 있는 8절지 종이를 나눠 주시고, 다음 날 물어 보니 그 여학생을 빼고는 다 앞자리를 기피했던 것이었다.

머리를 단아하게 묶은 이름도 모르고 성도 모르는 그 여학생은 사춘기의 나에

게는 연상의 여인이었다. 연상의 여인을 두고 자존심 상하게 뒷자리로 가기가 싫어 기초 문법도 모르는 채 무조건 하루에 20여 개의 문장을 외었다. 저녁에 암기하고도 불안해 엄마보고 새벽에 깨워 달라해 목욕재개 후 상쾌한 마음으로 다시 암기했다.

시간이 흘러 한 달이 다 되어 가자 선생님이 아직 중 2이니 한 달 더 들어보라고 권유하셔서 또 다음 달 등록을 했다. 기대한 대로 그 연상의 여학생도 앞줄에 앉아 있었다. 어찌나 기쁜지 또 미친 듯이 문장을 외어 500여 개 문장을 외우니 문법이 저절로 이해가 가기 시작했다.

내가 영어에 흥미를 갖게 한 선생님의 이름을 아직도 기억하고 있다 바로 권재열 선생님이다. 선생님 덕분에 아마 내가 수입부에서 업무를 원활히 처리하고, 유학도 가고, 10여 년 전 파고다 외국어학원에서 토익강의를 할 기회도 얻고, 이를 계기로 현 재직 중인 대학의 학과에 공무원 영어과목을 개설하고 토익책을 집필해 행정학과 학생들에게 공무원 시험의 당락을 결정짓는 영어를 가르칠 수 있고, 이번에는 행정학개론을 영어로 출간하게 되어 무척 행복하다.

이 책의 특징은 첫째, TOEIC 강의와 TOEIC 책 저술을 경험으로 행정학 원서강독을 토익 수준의 어휘와 문법을 위주로 집필하려고 시도한 것이다. 둘째, Part 1의 각 장 뒤에 TOEIC for Chapter와 Vocabulary for TOEIC을 넣어 학생들이 행정학을 영어로 공부하면서 TOEIC 대비도 자연스럽게 하도록 한 것이다. 셋째, 이해를 돕기 위해 다양한 그림과 표 등을 많이 사용하려고 노력했다.

모쪼록 영어로 행정학을 공부해 영어와 행정학이라는 두 마리의 토끼를 동시에 잡기를 바란다.

2016. 10
최 창 현

CONTENTS

Part 1 Fundamentals of Public Administration 9

Chapter 01 The Evolution of Public Administration 11

1. The Various Definitions of Public Administration / 12
2. Public Administration as an Interdisciplinary Science / 12

Chapter 02 The Roots of American Public Administration 18

1. Hamiltonian Classicism(Big Government) / 19
2. Jeffersonian Romanticism(Small Government) / 19
3. Madisonian Neoclassicism(Separation of Powers) / 20
4. Wilson's Efficient Government in Action / 20

Chapter 03 Paradigm 1: Politics/Adm. Dichotomy, 1880s~1910s 26

Chapter 04 Paradigm 2: The Principles of Public Administration, 1910s~1930s 36

Chapter 05 Paradigm 3: Politics/Adm. New Dichotomy, 1940s~1960s 51

Chapter 06 Paradigm 4: PA as Management, 1950s~1970s 58

Chapter 07 Paradigm 5: PA as Public Administration, 1970s~1990s 69

Chapter 08 Paradigm 6: From Government to Governance, 1990s~ 82

1. PA as Governance(1990s into the 2000) / 83

Chapter 09 Approaches to PA 90

1. Systems Theory / 91
2. Ecological Approach / 93
3. Behavioral Approach / 97
4. Public Choice Theory / 98

Part 2 Organizations 113

Chapter 01 Why Do We Need Organizations? 115

1. The Necessity of Organizations: From the View-point of Social Network Theory / 117

Chapter 02 The Definitions and Types of Organization 120

1. Traditional Definition of Organizations / 121
2. A New Interpretation of Organizations / 121

Chapter 03 The Changes of Organization Theory Paradigms 128

1. Closed System Theory: Classical Organization Theory and Neo-classical Organization Theory / 130
2. Open System Theory: Structural Contingency Theory / 146
3. Chaos Theory: Self-Organization / 152

Part 3 Public Policy 163

Chapter 01 The Definition and Process of Public Policy 165

1. The Definition of Public Policy / 166
2. The Process of Public Policy / 166
3. The Concepts in Public Policy / 175

Chapter 02 The Korean Public Policy 178

1. Public Policy in The Chosun Dynasty and in the Military Government / 179

2. Public Policy in Korea / 179

Part 4 Public Personnel Administration 185

Chapter 01 The Definition of Public Personnel Administration 187

Chapter 02 Inputs of Public Personnel Administration 189

1. Merit System vs. Spoils System / 190
2. Position Classification / 191

Chapter 03 Conversion Process in Personnel Administration 194

1. Recruitment / 195
2. Performance Appraisal / 195
3. Compensation / 195

Chapter 04 Outputs and Feedback in Public Personnel Administration 197

Part 5 Public Budgeting 201

Chapter 01 The Brief History of Budgeting 203

Chapter 02 The Public Budgeting Process 207

Appendix Public Administration Glossary of Terms 211

Index 229

Part 1 Fundamentals of Public Administration

"…*If the Government cannot create happiness for its people, there is no purpose for the Government to exist.*"

—Legal Code of Bhutan 1729, which is enshrined in the Constitution of 2008 the role of GNH is firmly established now at the heart of the nation and government.

In Part 1, we lay fundamental foundations on the basics related to public administration. In Chapter 1. we take a brief look at the various definitions of public administration, and also deal with how public administration has evolved since its birth.

In Chapter 2. the roots of American public administration such as; 1. Hamiltonian Classicism, 2. Jeffersonian Romanticism, and 3. Madisonian Neoclassicism are searched for.

And from Chapter 3 through Chapter 8, we try to trace back to the paradigms of public administration and to find out and retrospect how they have been changed in various ways, starting from 1900, paradigm of Politics/Administration Dichotomy to paradigm of governance in 1990s. Finally in Chapter 9, different approaches and theories to public administration are discussed.

01 Chapter

The Evolution of Public Administration

Public administration encompasses a complex set of interrelated concepts, thus a simple definition will not suffice. It draws from many different academic disciplines, includes a variety of agencies, and is linked closely to several distinct professions.

LEARNING OBJECTIVES

After reading Chapter 1 in the textbook, the student should be able to:

1. Define public administration.
2. Locate public administration within its interdisciplinary context.
3. Define the subject matter that forms the core of public administration.
4. Provide a brief background of the study of administration and its key early players.
5. Explain the real meaning of the politics-administration dichotomy.
6. Write short critical essays on major issues covered in the chapter.

1. The Various Definitions of Public Administration

Public administration(PA) is the implementation of government policy and also an academic discipline. It emphasizes the structure and process of bureaucratic organizations, including public policy, personnel, and budgeting. In this book due to the limits of space and the simplicity of the book, this book deals mainly with organizations.

The word 'administration' has been derived from Latin words 'ad' meaning 'to' and 'ministiare' meaning 'serve.' Thus the word administration means to execute the policy of government to serve citizens.

Now take a look at how scholars define Public Administration.

Denhardt(1995): Public Administration is concerned with the management of public programs.

Wilson(1887): Public Administration is the detailed and systematic execution of public law(administrative study is to discover first what government can properly and successfully do, and how it can do these proper things with the utmost possible efficiency and the least possible cost either of money or of energy).

Simon(1994): In its broadest sense, administration can be defined as the activities of groups cooperating to accomplish common goals.

Public administration 1) is a cooperative group effort in a public setting. 2) covers all three branches such as the executive, the legislative and the judicial and their interrelationships. 3) has an important role in the formulation of public policy, and is thus a part of the political process. 4) is different from private administration. 5) is closely associated with numerous private groups and individuals in providing services to the community(Nigro, Felix A, & Lloyd G. Nigro, 1989).

2. Public Administration as an Interdisciplinary Science

The scope of public administration is also various. In a narrow perspective, public administration is only the activities concerned with the executive branch of government.

The executive functions are POSDCoRB in terms of Gulick. P stands for planning, O stands for organizing, S stands for staffing, D stands for directing,

Co stands for Coordination, R stands for reporting, and B stands for budgeting.

Public administration, however in a rather broader sense, is an interdisciplinary science composed of many areas such as politics, law, business, and economics. At the intersection of public administration and politics there is public policy, at the intersection of public administration and law there is administrative law, at the intersection of public administration and business there is management, at the intersection of public administration and economics there is public choice.

Figure 1–1 Interdisciplinary Interface of Public Administration

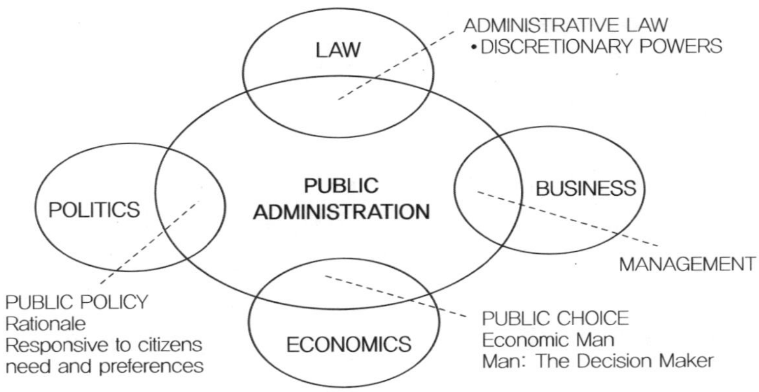

TOEIC for Chapter 1.

01 Thus the word administration means ______ the policy of government to serve citizens.

(A) executing (B) on executing
(C) for executing (D) to execute

Key Point

◆ **부정사와 동명사** ◆

문장에서 준 동사(부정사/동명사/분사)가 필요한 이유

우리가 가장 중요하게 생각해야 하는 것은 **문장이 하나면 본 동사로 반드시 하나**만 나와야 한다는 것이다. 이는 실제로 TOEIC 시험 문제를 푸는 데 있어서 가장 기본이 되는 원리라고 말할 수 있다. 그러나 사실상 문장이 조금만 길어지면 동사 하나만을 가지고 쓸 수 있는 문장은 거의 없다. 따라서 이럴 경우에는 여러 동사 중 본동사 하나를 제외한 나머지 동사를 **동사의 기능은 하지만 외관상의 품사는 동사가 아닌** 부정사(공식적인 품사는 명사, 형용사, 부사 중 하나임)나 동명사(품사는 명사) 또는 분사(품사는 형용사)의 꼴로 쓰면 되는 것이다. 결국, 위와 같은 준동사가 없는 문장은 거의 없다고 할 수 있기 때문에 TOEIC 문법에서 가장 중요한 자리를 차지한다고 말할 수 있다.

[부정사] – 형태는 To+동사원형(Root)이고 품사는 일정하게 정해져 있지 않다. 즉, 문장 상황에 따라 품사가 달라진다. 명사, 형용사, 부사 중 하나이다.

To study mathematics is hard. (명사)
She has a lot of reading materials to read. (형용사)
She is going abroad to study public administration. (부사)

[동명사] – 형태는 동사원형(Root)+ing이고 품사는 명사이다.

해설 부정사만을 목적어로 취하는 동사

▶기타 부정사를 목적어로 취하는 동사들: Piano

plan(~할 계획이다), intend, agree(동의하다), need(필요로 하다), offer(제안하다) hope / wish / want / desire(바라다, 소망하다), manage(이럭저럭 ~하다), afford(~할 여력이 있다), attempt(시도하다), refuse(거부하다), ask / demand(요구하다),

learn(~하게 되다), deserve(~받을 가치가 있다), pretend(~인 척하다), mean(의미하다), threaten(위협하다)
따라서 답은 (D) to execute

02 Now ____ a look at how scholars define Public Administration.

(A) make (B) take (C) put (D) bring

해설 두 단어 동사(Two-word verb): 동사+전치사 관용구에 유의
look 같은 쉬운 동사일수록 잘 정리해 두어야 한다.
look(at=see, for=find out, into=investigate, around, over, to=rely on, after=inquire after)
Look at me.=Take a look at me.
The detective is looking into the accident.
세 단어 동사(Three-word verb): 동사+전치사+전치사 관용구에 유의
look up to=respect, look down on=despise, look forward to=long for
I look up to my father.=I respect my father.
I look to my father.=I rely on my father.
따라서 답은 (B) take

03 Public Administration is an interdisciplinary science composed ____ many areas such as politics, law, business, and economics.

(A) of (B) from (C) by (D) with

해설 ~로 구성되다 be composed of=consist of=be made up of=comprise
(which is) composed of 관계대명사 주격과 be 동사는 생략 가능
따라서 답은 (A) of

04 P stands ____ planning.

(A) out (B) for (C) up (D) by

해설 stand by
(방관·좌시하며) 가만히[그냥] 있다
How can you stand by and see him accused of something he didn't do?

stand by somebody (어려운 상황에서도) ~의 곁을 지키다
Famous song, 'Stand by your man.'

stand out (as something) (~로서) 두드러지다

Four points stand out as being more important than the rest.

stand up 서 있다
There were no seats left so I had to stand up.
stand for=represent 대변하다
따라서 답은 (B) for

05 **Public Administration is concerned ____ the management of public programs.**

(A) about (B) in (C) on (D) with

해설 전치사에 따라 의미가 달라지는 동사에 유의
be concerned with (=have interest in) ~에 관심이 있다
I'm concerned with Public Administration.

be concerned about (=be anxious about) ~을 걱정하다
I'm concerned about his health.
따라서 답은 (D) with

06 **Administrative study is to discover first ____ government can properly and successfully do.**

(A) which (B) that (C) of which (D) what

해설 관계대명사 What
◇ 관계대명사 what은 선행사를 포함한다: what=선행사+관계대명사
what은 that which~, all that~, anything that~, the thing which~와 같은 용법이다.
∴ what은 자체 내에 선행사와 관계대명사가 포함되었으며 명사절을 유도한다.
* What one has: 재산, What one is: 인격
◇ You should judge a man ***not*** by what he has ***but*** by what he is.
* ***What***(that which) ***is beautiful*** is not always good. (주어[명사절])
* I will do ***what***(=all that) I can. (목적어[명사절])
따라서 답은 (D) what

Vocabulary for TOEIC

1. evolution
2. definition
3. administration
4. interdisciplinary
5. fundamental = basic
6. foundation
7. deal with = treat
8. trace
9. find out = search
10. implementation
11. government
12. policy
13. discipline
14. mean = intend
15. means and ends
16. execute
17. proper = appropriate
18. successfully
19. successively
20. intersection
21. discretionary
22. responsive
23. acronym

References

Denhardt, Robert B.(1995). *Public Administration: An Action Orientation*. Second Edition Wadsworth Publishing Company, Belmont, CA.

McCurdy, Howard E.(1977). *Public Administration: A Synthesis*. Cummings Publishing Company, Menlo Park, CA.

Nicolas, Henry(1980). *Paradigms of Public Administration*. University of Georgia.

Nigro, Felix A, & Lloyd G. Nigro(1989). *Modern Public Administration*, 7th ed., Harper & Row.

Shafritz, Jay M.(1988). *The Dorsey Dictionary of American Government and Politics*. The Dorsey Press, Chicago, IL.

Simon, Herbert A.(1994). *Administrative behavior; How organizations can be understood in terms of decision making process*. Roskide: Roskide University Press.

Wilson, Woodrow(1887). The Study of Public Administration. *Political Science Quartly*, II(2).

02 Chapter The Roots of American Public Administration

The care of human life and happiness is the first and only legitimate objective of good government.

—Thomas Jefferson, 3rd President of the United States

LEARNING OBJECTIVES

After reading Chapter 2 in the textbook, the student should be able to:

1. Understand the roots of American public administration.
2. Wilson's Understand the Efficient Government in action shown and manifested in his book, The Study of Public Administration.

The roots of American public administration can be roughly grouped into four categories; 1. Hamiltonian Classicism, 2. Jeffersonian Romanticism, 3. Madisonian Neoclassicism, and 4. Wilson's Efficient Government in Action.

1. Hamiltonian Classicism(Big Government)

Alexander Hamilton

The root of Hamiltonian Federalism was a big and strong central government. To him, the Constitution was a charter binding the states to create a stable union. This stability depended, in this perspective on the national government possessing more power than the individual states.

Hamilton and the Federalists wanted the young nation to become a manufacturing empire to sustain economic growth. Hamilton called for tariffs, or taxes placed on foreign goods to raise the price, to encourage manufacturing and make American produced goods more affordable. This British model of economic growth worried Jefferson who saw the potential for America becoming a nation of urban dwellers.

2. Jeffersonian Romanticism(Small Government)

Thomas Jefferson

It is also called as Jeffersonian Republicanism. Jefferson abhorred the idea of America becoming an urban, manufacturing nation, something that could happen rapidly under the Hamiltonian vision. Instead, he believed rural individualism, symbolized by the small–scale independent farmer who owns his own small land, was the best way to sustain a republic. They were the exemplars of American virtue, he claimed.

3. Madisonian Neoclassicism(Separation of Powers)

James Madison

The Madisonian Model is a fundamental philosophy of Presidential conduct that adheres primarily to the implied and denoted powers of the executive branch in the U.S. Constitution. First exhibited by James Madison, the model is a philosophy of the use of the presidential powers. The Madisonian model is a structure of government in which the powers of the government are separated into three branches: the executive, the legislative, and the judicial.

These ideas from Madison on the separation of powers along with his theory of checks and balances were not new. In 1748, French philosopher Baron de Montesquieu described these concepts in his book The Spirit of the Laws. Here Montesquieu explained how these checks on powers were efficient in preventing tyranny.

4. Wilson's Efficient Government in Action

Wilson believed that the study of public administration could enable officials to increase governmental efficiency. Therefore, he suggested the distinction between politics and administration be politics–free and that "the field of administration be the field of business"; thus, establishing what became known as the "politics–administration" dichotomy.

Wilson argued that administration is the most obvious part of the Government and the least discussions happen around it. He further says that despite being the executive, the operative and the most visible side of the Government and being as old as the Government itself it has remain hidden from the inspection and scrutiny of writer, authors and subject matter experts where it should have been the centre of debates and researches.

Wilson had carefully studied the administrative practices of not just France and England but a small nation like Prussia, and he praised the ruler Frederick the Great who regarded himself as the chief servant of the people and his office as a public trust.

To sum up, Wilson proposed a very senseful and businesslike approach to administration which should be free of political doctrines. We cannot over-estimate the famous and pioneering work of Wilson the study of public administration. So let's scan it.

Excerpts 1: The Study of Public Administration by Woodrow Wilson

Woodrow Wilson

I suppose that no practical science is ever studied where there is no need to know it. The very fact, therefore, that the eminently practical science of administration is finding its way into college courses in this country would prove that this country needs to know more about administration, were such proof of the fact required to make out a case.

It need not be said, however, that we do not look into college programmes for proof of this fact. It is a thing almost taken for granted among us, that the present movement called civil service reform must, after the accomplishment of its first purpose, expand into effors to improve, not the personnel only, but also the organization and methods of our government offices: because it is plain that their organization and methods need improvement only less than their personnel.

It is the object of administrative study to discover, first, what government can properly and successfully do, and secondly, how it can do these proper things with the utmost possible efficiency and at the least possible cost either of money or of energy. On both these points there is obviously much need of light among us; and only careful study can supply that light.

Before entering on that study, however, it is needful:

Ⅰ. The History of Public Administration Study

To take some account of what others have done in the same line; that is to say, of the history of the study.

1. To ascertain just what is its subject-matter.
2. To determine just what are the best methods by which to develop it,

and the most clarifying political conceptions to carry with us into it.

Unless we know and settle these things, we shall set out without chart or compass.

The science of administration is the latest fruit of that study of the science of politics which begun some twenty-two hundred years ago. It is a birth of our own century, almost of our own generation.

Why was it so late in coming? Why did it wait till this too busy century of ours to demand attention for itself? Administration is the most obvious part of government; it is government in action; it is the executive, the operative, the most visible side of government, and is of course as old as government itself. It is government in action, and one might very naturally expect to find that government in action had arrested the attention and provoked the scrutiny of writers of politics very early in the history of systematic thought.

But such was not the case. No one wrote systematically of administration as a branch of the science of government until the present century had passed its first youth and had begun to put forth its characteristic flower of systematic knowledge. ……

Ⅱ. The Subject of Public Administration Study

The field of administration is the field of business. ……

Ⅲ. The Method of Public Administration Study

Let it be noted that it is the distinction, already drawn, between administration and politics which makes the comparative method so safe in the field of administration.

When we study the administrative systems of France and Germany, knowing that we are not in search of political principles, we need not care a peppercorn for the constitutional or political reasons which Frenchmen or Germans give for their practices when explaining them to us.

If I see a murderous fellow sharpening a knife cleverly, I can borrow his way of sharpening the knife without borrowing his probable intention to commit murder with it; …… By keeping this distinction in view, we are on perfectly safe ground, and can learn without error what foreign systems have to teach us. ……

TOEIC for Chapter 2.

01 Hamilton wanted the young nation to become a manufacturing empire to sustain ______ growth.

(A) economical (B) economic
(C) economy (D) economically

02 Japan is expected to increase its ______ assistance to developing countries.

(A) economical (B) economic
(C) economically (D) economy

해설 economical = 절약하는 My wife is very economical.
economic = 경제의 경제원조 = economic assistance 경제성장 = economic growth
따라서 1번과 2번 답은 (B) economic

03 Hamilton called for tariffs, or taxes placed on foreign goods to raise the price, to encourage manufacturing and make American produced goods ______.

(A) afford (B) affordable
(C) most affordable (D) more affordable

해설 가격이 적당한 = affordable
His prices are affordable. 가격이 알맞은 식품 = affordable foods

[동사](수동태로는 안 씀. 특히, 부정문이나 의문문에서 보통 can, could, be able to 와 함께 쓰여)(…을 살 · 할 · 금전적 · 시간적) 여유[형편]가 되다

Can we afford a new car? 우리가 새 차를 살 여유가 되요?

Hamilton called for tariffs, or taxes placed on foreign goods to raise the price, to encourage manufacturing and make American produced goods more affordable. 제조업을 장려하고 미국산 제품이 좀 더 가격이 알맞은 제품이 되도록 외국제품에 부과되는 관세나 세금의 인상을 요청하였다.

called for = request = demand = 요구하다
The situation calls for prompt action. 상황이 즉각적인 조처를 요한다.

call off=cancel=취소하다 He called off the meeting.

비교구문과 배수

1. 규칙변화
① 일음절어
 * hard－harder－hardest
 * long－longer－longest
 ◇ 단모음+단자음의 경우는 자음을 하나 더 쓰고 －er, －est를 붙임.
 * big－bigger－biggest
② －le, －ly, －some, －ow, －er 등의 어미로 끝나는 2음절어
 * able－abler－ablest
 * early－earlier－earliest
③ more, the most
 : a, e i, o, u 등의 모음이 3음절 이상의 형용사인 difficult, beautiful, diligent, interesting 등과 2음절어로서 어미가 －ful, －able, －less, －ous, －ive, －ing 등으로 끝나는 단어는 more, the most를 붙여서 비교급과 최상급을 만듦.
difficult, more difficult, the most difficult
affordable은 3음절이어서 more를 붙임.
따라서 답은 (D) more affordable

04 **This project is one of the _____ tasks that we have ever undertaken.**

(A) challenged (B) challenging
(C) most challenging (D) more challenging

해설 one of 다음은 복수 중에 하나임으로 복수 명사가 나오고 최상급이 나옴.
예를 들어, 이 영화는 내가 이제까지 본 영화 중에 가장 재미있는 영화 중에 하나이다.
This movie is one of the most interesting movies that I have ever seen.
따라서 답은 (C) most challenging

Vocabulary for TOEIC

1. stability
2. dweller
3. urban
4. depend on = rely on
5. perspective
6. abhor = dislike
7. exemplar = good model = good mirror = good example
8. checks and balances
9. adhere = to stick to = cling to
10. separation
11. tyranny
12. dichotomy
13. eminently
14. practical
15. proof
16. expand
17. take account of
18. ascertain = confirm the fact, find out, figure out
19. provoke
20. pioneer
21. enable officials to increase
22. scrutiny = investigation = perusal
23. scan = glance over = skim over = look over

References

Wilson, Woodrow(1887). The Study of Public Administration. *Political Science Quartly*, Ⅱ(2).

Jefferson, Thomas, et. al.(1976). *The Declaration of Independence.*

03
Chapter

Paradigm 1: Politics/Adm. Dichotomy, 1880s~1910s

The field of administration is the field of business.

—Woodrow Wilson

LEARNING OBJECTIVES

After reading Chapter 3 in the textbook, the student should be able to:

1. Understand the meaning of the Politics/Administration Dichotomy.
2. Understand the three schools of thought on the Politics/Administration Dichotomy, which are called, the separation, political, and interaction schools.

Paradigms of public administration have been changed in various ways, starting from 1900, paradigm of Politics/Adm. Dichotomy to paradigm of governance in 1990.

Woodrow Wilson and Frank Goodnow provided the rationale for public administration to be an academic discipline. Politics administration dichotomy has provoked long-running debates which persist until today. It may be argued though that the dichotomy is artificial and that power and partisan politics have had an influence upon the workings of public administration (Goodnow, 1900).

Politics versus Administration

Before we look into further it is best to differentiate first politics from administration. For President Wilson, the field of politics aims to answer the question, "Who shall make law and what shall it be?" while administration attempts to address the question, "How should the law be administered?" Using the similar line of thought, legal scholar and Wilson's contemporary Goodnow stated that while politics has something to do with policies or expressions of the State's will, administration has to do with the execution of such policies. Wilson and Goodnow made clear that politics is limited to crafting of policies and lawmaking, a function generally given to a State's legislative body; and administration is focused on the implementation of laws, a function normally held by the State's executive branch.

Although these definitions are valid, it would be somewhat problematic if we were to use this in our present (or any future) analysis. Other than the overlapping (if not harmony) of functions of politics and administration, the problem which now remains is that this longstanding differentiation of these fields became out of date.

In modern usage, public administration is not anymore a practice restricted to the domain of executive branch. In the passage of time, it became more concerned with serving the public through formulation of necessary laws, initiating and proactive implementation of laws crafted, and efficient delivery of public services.

During the past decades, public administration scholars proposed numerous explanations and theoretical models in their attempts to understand the role of public administration in the political process. We examine these scholarly efforts under three schools of thought, which are called, the separation, political, and interaction schools.

The Separation School

We use the term "separation" to denote this school of thought in that a group of scholars advance an agenda for separating politics from administration to the extent possible for both normative and practical reasons. The separation scholars tend to view the governmental realm as divided into two zones, that is, politics and administration.

They take a functional approach to analyze the relationship between politics and administration. The function of politics is to provide guidance, or what Wilson(1887) said, "setting the task for administration." The function of public administration, on the other hand, is to provide neutral competence to the policy process.

Bureaucratic neutrality covers both political and policy neutrality. More specifically, neutrality means that public employees and activities be non-partisan, apolitical, administering the public affairs with efficiency and loyalty to the elected leadership, without participating in or allowing their work to be affected by fighting and competing programs or partisans, and "maintaining a neutral stand on policy issues that divide the community."

The Political School

The political school represents a group of public administration scholars that emphasize and support a broad policy role for public administration. This school positions itself against the separation school and is characterized by total and outright rejection of the politics-administration distinction. The political school proponents consider public administration as an inseparable part of the political process.

The political school takes administrative discretion as a point of departure to rationalize the policy role of public administrators. Of many reasons, vague and ambiguous legislations, lack of technical knowledge and resources available to elected officials, and difficulties in monitoring and controlling bureaucratic behavior are a few used to signify the critical role of public administrators in the policy process. Consequently, for political school proponents, there are strong grounds to view public administrators as policy makers.

Some public administration scholars, representing the political school, rest their arguments on pragmatic grounds. In their view, political power in the U.S. governmental structure is widely diffused, and this fact makes it essential for public administrators to engage in politics, and build and maintain coalitions.

The Interaction School

The interaction school is represented by a group of public administration scholars that emphasize a high degree of collaboration between elected and administrative career officials while maintaining each one's traditional roles and unique perspectives.

As we all should know by now, politics and administration are inseparably intermixed. Both are central to effective actions. One problem is to bring them together in a symbiotic association yet keep each in its proper place. The other is to understand that the "proper place" of each will vary through time. There is no permanent solution, no fixed paradigm, to this or any other ends–means continuum.

In the ideal world of political–administrative world, as envisioned by the interaction school, public administrators maintain a productive partnership with elected officials, partnering with, informing and helping them in the policy process, yet remain accountable and responsive to their elected officials.

This phenomenon is called iron triangle, which means the policy–making relationships among the congressional committees, the bureaucracy, and interest groups. This notion of iron triangle can be applied to many such issues as political bargainings, the military–industrial complex, and Sewol Ferry Disaster to name a few.

The figure below displays the concept. At one corner of the triangle are interest groups (constituencies) who are the powerful interest's groups that influence Congressional votes in their favor and can sufficiently influence the re–election of a member of Congress in return for supporting their programs.

At another corner lay members of Congress who also seek to align themselves with a constituency for political and electoral support. These congressional members support legislation that advances the interest group's agenda by means of log-rolling and pork-barrelling.

Occupying the third corner of the triangle are bureaucrats, who are often pressured and often captured by the same powerful interest groups which their agency is designated to regulate.

The result is a three reciprocal way stable alliance that is sometimes called a sub-government because of its durability, impregnability, and power to determine policy strongly like an iron. An iron triangle(subgovernment) can result in the passing of very narrow, pork-barrel policies that benefit a small segment of the population.

Figure 3-1 Iron Triangle(Subgovernment) Diagram

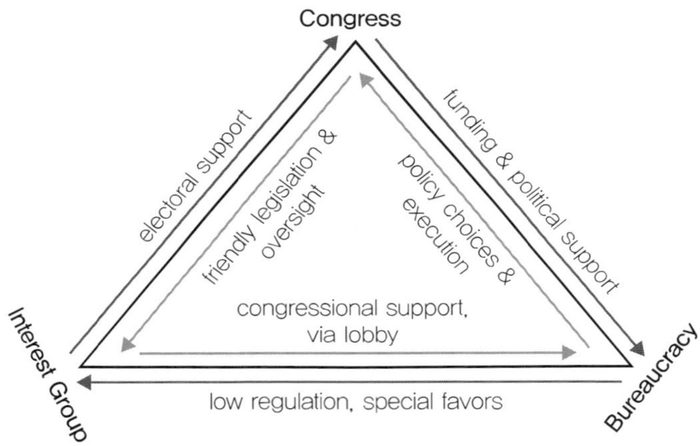

Source: http://www.omsj.org/issues/the-pharmaceutical-iron-triangle

In brief, the separation, political, and interaction schools each contributed immensely to our understanding of how public administrators are related to political process in contemporary government. Defining the role of public administration in the political process is a challenging academic task given the fact that any definition is likely to carry strong implications for the intellectual identity and institutional development of public administration. Decades of research produced a huge literature with important findings and insights. Yet, it is hard to conclude that the controversy is over.

Table 3-1 The Three Schools of Politics/P.A Dichotomy in Summary

Dimension	Separation School	Political School	Interaction School
Politics-Administration distinction	Dichotomous	Undistinguishable	Overlaps
Nature of relationship between elected and administrative officials	Superior-Subordinate	Equals/Competitive	Partnership/Complimentarity (elected officials are senior partners)
The assumption on governance	Consensus	Conflict	Conflict(can be contained through cooperation)
Public administrators' policy role	Policy advising to elected officials, policy implementation	Policy formulation, policy implementation, policy evaluation	Policy formulation(excluding setting broad goals/mission), policy implementation, policy evaluation

Source: Tansu Demir, Politics and Administration: A Review of Research and Some Suggestions.

Even though the dichotomy between politics and administration is one of the oldest issues in public administration, it continues to hold great relevance for administrators today. You will recall that an early essay by Woodrow Wilson framed the study of public administration. In addition to his emphasis on businesslike practices, Wilson was concerned with isolating the processes of administration from politics.

With respect to this issue, Wilson wrote, "Administration lies outside the proper sphere of politics. Administrative questions are not political questions." In other words, while policies were to be debated and decided by politicians, they were to be carried out by a politically neutral, professional bureaucracy. In this way, the everyday conduct of government would be isolated from the potentially corrupting influence of politics.

TOEIC for Chapter 3.

01 Power and partisan politics ______ a disproportionate influence upon the workings of public administration.

(A) make (B) take (C) have (D) do

해설 Chapter 1에서 설명한 바와 같이 동사를 다시 영어로 바꿔 사용하는 경향이 있다.
Look at me. = Take a look at me.
영향을 미치다라는 표현은 have를 사용
influence = have an influence on
impact = have an impact on
affect = have an effect on
따라서 답은 (C) have

02 Wilson suggested the distinction between politics and administration ______ politics-free and that the field of administration be the field of business.

(A) was (B) had been (C) be (D) were

03 The employees insisted that overtime hours ______ fully paid.

(A) am (B) were (C) be (D) is

Key Point

명령/요구/주장/제안의 동사문제는 일 년에 두 번 정도씩 꼭 출제가 된다.
요구하다 - ask, command, demand, require, request
주장하다 - insist
제안하다 - propose, suggest, recommend
명령하다 - order, command
+ that S + 동사원형(Root)
(이때 동사원형에는 should의 의미가 있다.)

해설 suggested가 과거이지만 that절의 동사는 원형이 온다.
따라서 2번과 3번 답은 (C) be

그러나 단순한 사실을 나타낼 경우는 동사원형을 사용하지 않고 시제의 일치에 따른다.
cf. Authors have insisted that dehumanization and specialization caused workers stress and ultimately alienation.

04 It would be somewhat problematic if we _____ to use this in our present analysis.

(A) was (B) were (C) had been (D) have

05 Had I known she was coming to Seoul, I ________ to the airport to meet her.

(A) would have gone (B) would go
(C) had gone (D) went

Key Point

◆ **가정법 응용** ◆
[TOEIC 시험에 나오는 가정법] - 가정법의 형태(시제)만 알면 대부분의 문제가 해결된다.
1. 가정법 현재 - If + S + 현재형 동사, S + will + Root(동사원형)
2. 가정법 미래 - If + S + Should + Root, S + will + Root
3. 가정법 과거 - If + S + 과거동사(be동사 → were), S + would/could/should/might + Root
4. 가정법 과거완료 - If + S + had + p.p, S + would/should/could/might + have + p.p

[예문을 통해서 각각의 차이점을 알아본다]
1. 가정법 현재: If I am a bird, I will reach you.
(잘 모르고 불확실한 사실에 대한 단순가정)
2. 가정법 미래: If I should be a bird, I will reach you. (강한 의심)
3. 가정법 과거: If I were a bird, I would reach you. (현재 사실의 반대)
4. 가정법 과거완료: If I had been a bird, I would have reached you.
(과거 사실에 대한 반대)

▸가정법 현재, 미래, 과거는 직설법으로는 전부 같은 시제이고 가정법 과거완료만이 유일한 과거 시제이다.

가정법 문제의 대부분은 시제 일치 문제이기 때문에 가정법의 시제 4가지만 정확하게 알면 70% 이상의 문제를 풀 수가 있다. 즉, 주절과 종속절 중 한쪽의 시제를 주고 다른 쪽의 시제를 구하라는 문제가 대부분의 가정법 문제이다(단, 가정법 미래 문제는 단순 시제를 묻는 기본형 가정법 문제로는 시험에 출제되지 않는다).

해설 위 문제는 가정법 과거를 질문하는 문제이다 – If + S + 과거동사(be동사 → were), S + would/could/should/might + Root

If절에는 동사의 과거형이 온다.

따라서 4번 답은 (B) were

◆가정법 응용◆

If의 생략

가정법에서 If는 생략이 가능하다. 단, If가 생략되면 문장의 주어와 동사가 도치가 된다는 점에 유의하자.

▸ 예: If I had been a bird, I would have reached you.
→ Had I been a bird, I would have reached you.

Had I known she was coming to Seoul은 If I had known~이므로 가정법 과거완료

따라서 5번 답은 (A) would have gone

Vocabulary for TOEIC

1. represent = stand for
2. interest group
3. consensus
4. conflict
5. overlap
6. separation
7. interaction
8. challenging
9. academic
10. task
11. recall
12. corrupt
13. phenomenon
14. initiating = proactive
15. analyze
16. competitive = fighting
17. political bargaining
18. the military – industrial complex
19. constituency = interest group and residents in the district
20. iron triangle = subgovernment

References

Clark, Cochran E. et. al.(2009). *American Public Policy.* Wadsworth Pub. Co.

Tansu Demir(2008). Politics and Administration: A Review of Research and Some Suggestions.

Wilson, Woodrow(1887). The Study of Public Administration, *Political Science Quartly,* Ⅱ(2).

http://www.omsj.org/issues/the – pharmaceutical – iron – triangle

04

Chapter

Paradigm 2: The Principles of Public Administration, 1910s~1930s

"Management in government is harder than in the private sector. There are many reasons for this: less clarity of direction, less control over resources, more relationships to maintain, fewer indications of success, less privacy, more influences to take into account in decision–making, less flexibility to motivate and reward subordinates."

—Timothy Plumtre

LEARNING OBJECTIVES

After reading Chapter 4 in the textbook, the student should be able to:

1. Understand the Principles of Scientific Management by Taylor.
2. Understand the bureaucratic theory by Weber.
3. Understand Gulick's POSDCoRB and Mayo's human relations theory.
4. Understand the administrative structure of the federal government, in particular the executive branch machinery.

The Principles of Scientific Management by Taylor

Frederick Taylor

People have been managing work for hundreds of years, and we can trace formal management ideas to the 20th century. One of the earliest of these theorists was Frederick Winslow Taylor. He started the Scientific Management movement, and he and his associates were the first people to study the work process scientifically. They studied how work was performed, and they looked at how this affected worker productivity.

This was very different from the way work was typically done in businesses beforehand. A factory manager at that time had very little contact with the workers, and he left them on their own to produce the necessary product. There was no standardization, and a worker's main motivation was often continued employment, so there was no incentive to work as quickly or as efficiently as possible.

Frederick Taylor, generally thought of as the father of scientific management, pioneered the development of scientific management based on the time and motion studies. He wrote the result of his studies in 1911 in the Principles of Scientific Management. And he is best known for his "one best way approach" in accomplishing task. It can be said that classical organization theory evolved from this notion.

Bureaucracy by Weber

Max Weber(1946), a German sociologist who is known as the Father of Modern Sociology, made a descriptive analysis of bureaucratic organizations. He presented some major variables or features of bureaucracy such as: hierarchy, division of labor, formally written rules and procedures, impersonality and neutrality; hence, providing a reference point in evaluating both the good and bad effects of bureaucratic structures(Weber, 1946; as cited in Shafritz & Hyde, 1997).

Bureaucracy means rule by officials, the administrative machinery of the state, and more broadly a legal, rational and rule-governed mode of organization. It is a government by a rigid hierarchy of bureaus, administrators, and officials characterized by excessive red tape, division of labor, specialization, vertical command and control, and organizational routines(http://www.thefreedictionary.com/bureaucracy).

Max Weber

POSDCoRB

Luther Gulick came up with a good administrative management principles and believed that adherence to a core set of these management principles would help organizations achieve optimum performance in working toward their goals. The principle of division of labor, for example, allows workers to develop expertise in performing particular tasks. In contrast, charging employees with a wide variety of unrelated duties inhibits the development of expertise.

Luther Gulick

The principle of unity of command cautions against directives coming from too many superiors because conflicting signals could arise and lead to confusion among employees.

A third principle, span of control, dictates that superiors should oversee a limited number of subordinates rather than a large number of subordinates. Monitoring and mentoring the work of subordinates is an easy task when the number of subordinates is small but becomes more difficult when superiors are charged with overseeing a large number of individuals. Management scholars claimed that the implementation of these and related principles would result in organizations characterized by an almost mechanical efficiency.

Another popular manifestation of this approach was that of Luther Gulick's POSDCoRB functions. Gulick and Urwick integrated the ideas of earlier theorists like Henri Fayol into a comprehensive theory of administration.

POSDCoRB was coined by Gulick with Urwick. It stands for the functions of management–planning, organizing, staffing, directing, coordinating, reporting & budgeting. POSDCoRB, however, was seen as less influential in post–war American government. Thereafter, Simon, Waldo and Appleby attacked the idea of POSDCoRB.

Appleby, led a postwar attack on the concept of politics–administration dichotomy by drafting a convincing case that "public administration was not something apart from politics" but rather at the "center of political life" (Stillman, 1991).

It is believed that a single science of administration, which exceeds the boundaries of the private and the public sector, exists. The reasoning of the science of administration was largely borrowed from Fayol's 14 principles of organization.

Management Principles

Henri Fayol

He synthesized the 14 principles of management. Here are some Management Principles developed by Henri Fayol:

- DIVISION OF WORK: Work should be divided among individuals and groups to ensure that effort and attention are focused on special portions of the task. Fayol presented work specialization as the best way to use the human resources of the organization.
- AUTHORITY: The concepts of Authority and responsibility are closely

related. Authority was defined by Fayol as the right to give orders and the power to obtain obedience. Responsibility involves being accountable, and is therefore naturally associated with authority. Whoever assumes authority also assumes responsibility.

- DISCIPLINE: A successful organization requires the common effort of workers. Penalties should be applied judiciously to encourage this common effort.
- UNITY OF COMMAND: Workers should receive orders from only one manager.
- UNITY OF DIRECTION: The entire organization should be moving towards a common objective in a common direction.
- SUBORDINATION OF INDIVIDUAL INTERESTS TO THE GENERAL INTERESTS: The interests of one person should not take priority over the interests of the organization as a whole.
- REMUNERATION(Rewards): Many variables, such as cost of living, supply of qualified personnel, general business conditions, and success of the business, should be considered in determining a worker's rate of pay.
- CENTRALIZATION: Fayol defined centralization as lowering the importance of the subordinate role. Decentralization is increasing the importance. The degree to which centralization or decentralization should be adopted depends on the specific organization in which the manager is working.
- SCALAR CHAIN: Managers in hierarchies are part of a chain like authority scale. Each manager, from the first line supervisor to the president, possess certain amounts of authority. Employees should be aware of where they stand in the organization's hierarchy, or chain of command.

  The President possesses the most authority; the first line supervisor the least. Lower level managers should always keep upper level managers informed of their work activities. The existence of a scalar chain and adherence to it are necessary if the organization is to be successful.
- EQUITY: All employees should be treated as equally as possible.
- STABILITY OF TENURE OF PERSONNEL: Retaining productive employees should always be a high priority of management.

- INITIATIVE: Management should take steps to encourage worker initiative, which is defined as new or additional work activity undertaken through self direction.
- ESPIRIT DE CORPS(Team Spirit): Management should encourage harmony and general good feelings among employees.

In the 1920s and early 1930s, Elton Mayo conducted the Hawthorne experiments on the theory of individuals within an organization which propelled the Human Relations School of Management thought.

Hawthorne experiments were conducted from 1927 to 1932 at the Western Electric Hawthorne Works in a suburb of Chicago, Illinois. The factory employed mainly women workers who assembled telephone cabling equipment. The aim of the studies was to establish the impact of different conditions of work on employee productivity. Initially, Mayo examined the affect of changes in the factory environment such as lighting and humidity. He then went on to study the effect of changes in employment arrangements such as breaks, hours, and managerial leadership. Not only were the Hawthorne experiments the first large-scale studies of working people's conditions ever made; they also produced a range of remarkable results that changed the face of people management.

The Astonishing Results of the Relay Assembly Room Experiments

Although Elton Mayo and his team conducted the Hawthorne Experiments over a number of years, it is his work with 6 women workers in the relay assembly room that made his name. Throughout the series of experiments, one of Mayo's team sat with the girls as they worked, noting everything they did, keeping them up-to-date with the experiment, asking for clarification, and listening to their views. The experiment began by introducing carefully controlled changes, each of which was continued for a test period of 4 to 12 weeks. The results of these changes were as follows:

- under normal conditions, with a 48-hour week, including Saturdays, and no breaks, the girls produced 2,400 relays a week each.
- they were then put on piece-work for 8 weeks. Output went up.
- two 5-minute rest pauses, morning and afternoon, were introduced for

a period of 5 weeks. Output went up once more.

- the rest pauses were lengthened to 10 minutes each. Output went up sharply.
- six 5–minute pauses were introduced, and the girls complained that their work rhythm was broken by the frequent pauses. Output fell slightly.
- the 2 rest pauses were re–instated, the first with a hot meal supplied by the Company free of charge. Output went up.
- the girls finished at 4 : 30 pm instead of 5 : 00 pm. Output went up.
- the girls finished at 4 : 00 pm. Output remained the same.
- finally, all the improvements were taken away, and the girls went back to the same conditions that they had at the beginning of the experiment: work on Saturday, 48–hour week, no rest pauses, no piece work and no free meal. These conditions lasted for a period of 12 weeks. Output was the highest ever recorded with the girls averaging 3,000 relays a week each.

It took Elton Mayo some time to work through the results of his Hawthorne Experiments, particularly the seemingly illogical results of the Relay Assembly room experiments. His main conclusion was that the prevailing view of the time, that people went to work purely for money and a living, was deeply flawed. Work was much more. It was first and foremost a group activity in which other people and their behaviour, be they colleagues, managers or observers, affected how well people worked. People's morale and productivity were affected not so much by the conditions in which they worked but by the recognition they received. The rises in productivity in the Relay Assembly Room were achieved under the interested eye of the observers not because the conditions made the workers feel good but because the workers felt valued.

Chester Barnard(1938) presented a more comprehensive theory of organizational behavior when he wrote the functions of the executive. He argued that for the executive to become more effective, he maintain an equilibrium between the needs of the employees and the organization.

His concepts were later explored and developed into more comprehensive theories and principles as advocated by other researches in organizational behavior and management, such as Herzberg's "motivation hygiene theory," Mc Gregor's "Theory X and Y," Argyris' "personality versus organization" and "Likert's Systems 1 to 4," and so on(Shafritz & Hyde, 1997).

Maslow(1943), on the other hand, focused on the hierarchical needs of the individual. His "theory of human motivation," states that the human being has five sets of needs: physiological, safety, love or affiliation, esteem and ultimately, and self-actualization. Theories related to organization will be dealt with in detail later in Part 2.

Basic Structures of Public Administration

The principles of organization are stated in many ways and there can be contradictions. They are essentially guidelines and are built around a few essentials. For example, administrative agencies may be organized by purpose, process, clientele or geographical divisions. In organizing agencies, consideration needs to be given to span of control, the scalar principle and the unity of command.

Other elements to consider include technical efficiency, the commensurability between responsibility and authority and specialization and coordination. These principles are neither mutually exclusive, nor capable of application to all situations without adaptation. Nonetheless, they are extremely useful for those engaged in organizational design or reorganization strategies.

We have an executive branch with the bureaucracy at its core. We have a legislature. We have a judiciary. We have electoral processes and procedures. We have sub-national institutions and local governments, together with decentralization processes and procedures.

Departmentation

In organizational matters, public administration has focussed on departmentation. A department is commonly defined as a major unit of government, usually entrusted with the management of a single substantive function. When headed by a minister (political executive) it is called a ministry.

Conventional wisdom required that the number of major departments be kept small. Some have insisted on a number between six and ten to enable the chief executive to effectively supervise and coordinate the affairs of government.

On the other hand, there are the political realities of developing countries, where coalition building produces a large number of departments so that each minister (coalition partner) can be accommodated. It is not uncommon to find examples of governments that have thirty to forty ministers like Cambodia.

The following depicts the departments of the Korean Government.

Figure 4–1 Office of the President

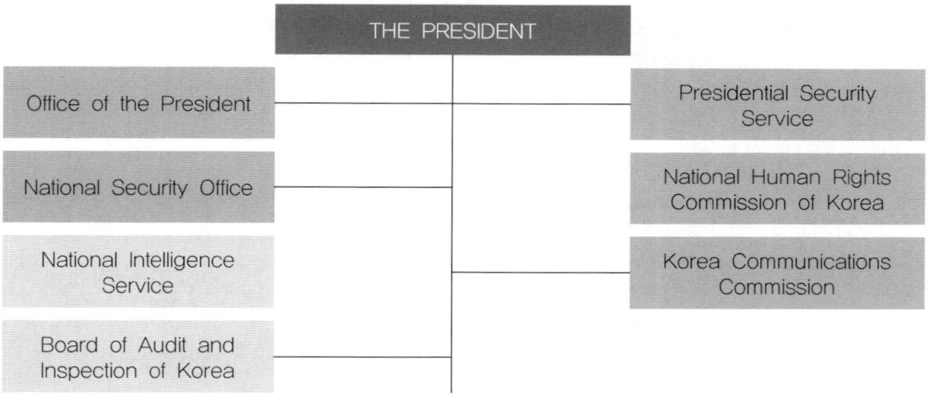

Figure 4–2 The Prime Minister

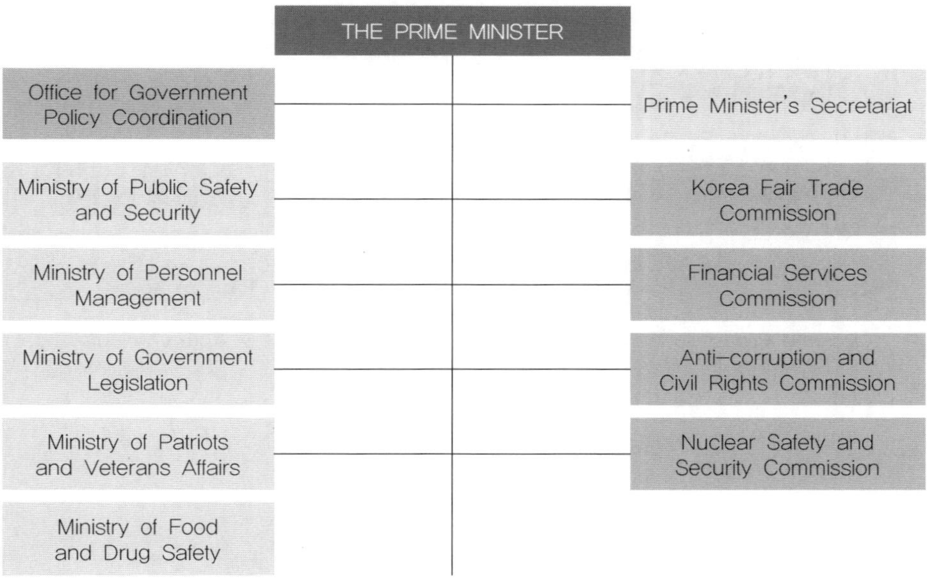

Figure 4–3 The Executive Branch

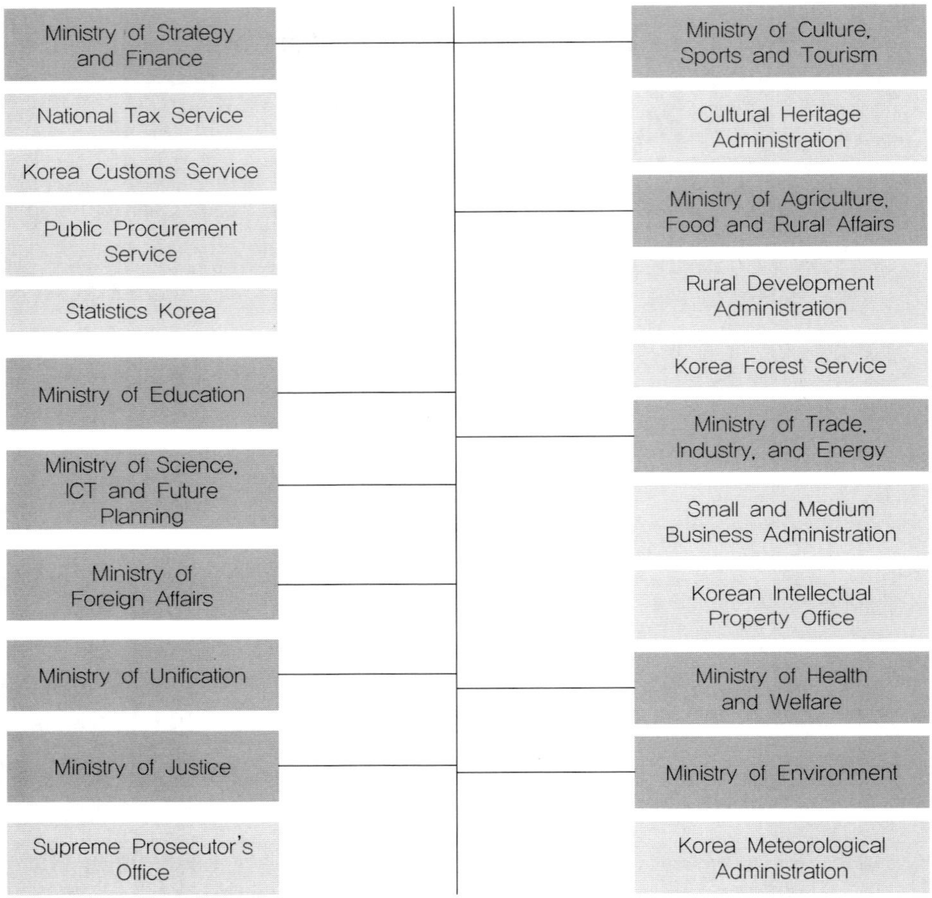

Figure 4-4 Continued

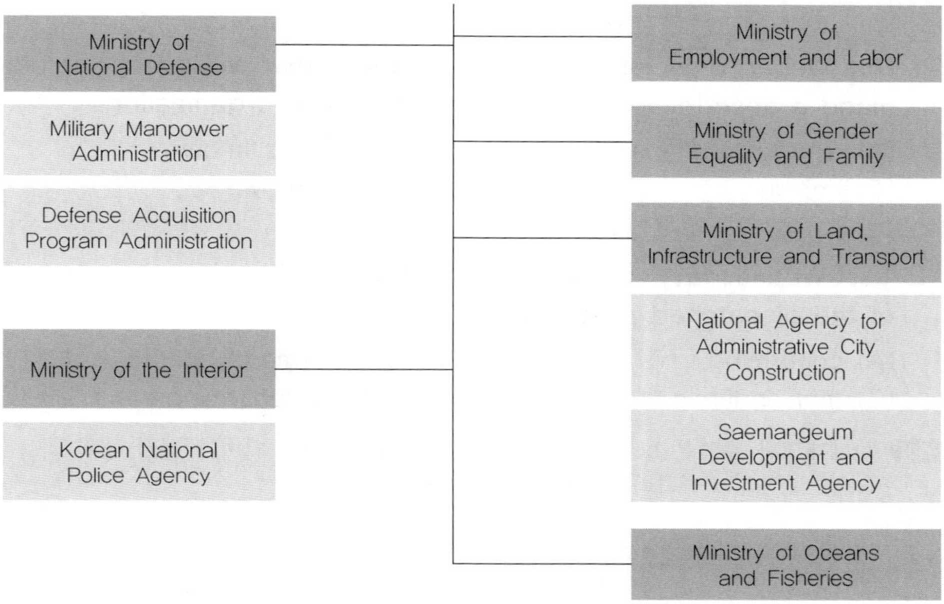

TOEIC for Chapter 4.

01 Max Weber, a sociologist ______ as the Father of Modern Sociology, made a descriptive analysis of bureaucratic organizations.

(A) who known (B) which is known

(C) known (D) that known

02 Last Wednesday, our department got a letter ______ the safe arrival of the dispatched products.

(A) confirming (B) confirmed

(C) that confirms (D) from confirming

해설 관계대명사 주격은 be 동사와 같이 나오면 be 동사의 의미가 없어 생략 가능 (who is) known 따라서 1번 답은 (C) known

(which is) confirming 따라서 2번 답은 (A) confirming

03 Another popular manifestation of this approaches was _____ of Luther Gulick's POSDCORB functions.

(A) this (B) these (C) those (D) that

해설 앞 단어를 다시 받는 용어는 단수일 경우 that, 복수일 경우 those이다. 따라서 답은 (D) that

04 The aim of the studies _____ to establish the impact of different conditions of work on employee productivity.

(A) were (B) was (C) will (D) have been

Key Point

TOEIC 시험에서 많이 출제가 되는 문제를 들라면 바로 수의 일치 문제를 들 수가 있다. 이는 **모든 시험에** 100% 출제가 되는데 특히, Part 6 문제로 출제가 된다. 따라서 Part 6 문제를 풀 때는 항상 동사가 틀릴 가능성이 있다고 생각하고, 제일 먼저 그 **동사의 주어가 무엇인지**를 찾아내면 대부분의 수의 일치 문제를 해결할 수 있다.

▸주어와 동사가 수식어구 등에 의해서 떨어져 있는 경우가 가장 많이 출제된다.

05 **The number of employees fired by the firm on a yearly basis ______ gradually decreasing.**

(A) are (B) is (C) be (D) have been

해설 주어가 studies가 아니라 The aim이므로 따라서 4번 답은 (B) was

주어가 employees가 아니라 The number이므로 따라서 5번 답은 (B) is

The number of employees 대신 A number of employees라면
A number of는 many의 의미로 형용사이므로 employees가 주어이다.

Vocabulary for TOEIC

1. hierarchy
2. division of labor
3. impersonality
4. neutrality
5. focus on
6. authority
7. hygiene
8. absorb
9. comprehensive
10. equipment
11. remuneration = rewards
12. avoid
13. threat
14. conduct
15. assemble
16. prevail = spread widely
17. state = declare = say
18. physiological
19. safety
20. affiliation
21. esteem
22. actualization
23. discourse = discussion = talk

References

Gulick, Luther(1937). "Science, Values and Public Administration." Papers on the Science of Administration.

Gulick, Luther, & Lyndall Urwick, eds.(1937). *Papers on the Science of Administration.* Institute of Public Administration, Columbia University.

Mayo, Elton G.(2003). *The Human Problems of an Industrial Civilization.* Routledge, reprint edition.

Pfeffer, Jeffrey(1982). *Organizations and Organization Theory.* Boston: Pitman.

Taylor, Frederick W.(1967). *The Principles of Scientific Management.* New York: W. W. Norton & Company.

Thompson, James D.(1967). *Organizations in Action.* New York: McGraw-Hill.

Weber, Max(1947). *The Theory of Social and Economic Organization.* trans, A. M. Parsons & T. Parsons. New York: Free Press.

05
Chapter

Paradigm 3: Politics/Adm. New Dichotomy, 1940s~1960s

Though government has an important role to play in meeting the many challenges that remain before us, we are coming to understand that no organization, including government, will fully succeed without the active participation of each of us. Volunteers are vital to enabling this country to live up to the true promise of its heritage.

— Bill Clinton, 42nd President of the United States

LEARNING OBJECTIVES

After reading Chapter 5 in the textbook, the student should be able to:

1. Understand the comparative administration and development administration.
2. Understand the criticism made by Simon on the classical management principles.

"A school of thought which began studying the role and problems of administration in developing countries calls its field Comparative Public Administration(CPA). Comparative Public Administration(CPA) is the comparative study of institutions, process, and behaviors in many contexts such as societal values, norms, religion, political culture, and economy."

In 1962, the Ford Foundation presented the Comparative administration Group, special division of the American Society for Public Administration (ASPA), with one-half million dollars to study methods for improving public administration in developing countries.

Public administration had passed recently through a period of widespread optimism about the power of administrative reform. Many practitioner-scholars believed that administration could be improved through the implementation of correct principles.

Around 80 some years earlier Luther Gulick had suggested that experts were on the verge of discovering principles of administration as immutable as the laws of physics and chemistry. Scholars had rediscovered Woodrow Wilson's dictum that good administrative practices did not depend upon the type of regimen which they were practiced.

Development Administration(DA) as a field of study emerged in 1950s as a convenient way to describe the new roles of the State and public administration in national progress and modernization of the developing countries. In contrast to law and order administration, the aim of development administration was change and innovation.

These developing countries endeavored to make efforts to be recognized as "emerging nations" and to recover and resurrect themselves after World War II. These countries were "concerned with increasing the capacity of the state to produce goods and services to meet and induce changing demands."

The United States had achieved great success in reconstructing the economies of Europe and Asia through instruments such as the Marshall Plan, which was a good example of CPA and DA.

In sum CPA cannot be disentangled from politics. politics is a key intervening variable. Thus, cross comparison of different political structure become essential to advance the knowledge and practice of PA.

Khator(1998) however, argued that DA was built upon several critical assumptions that: (1) development needs are the most important needs of developing countries, (2) the development needs of developing and developed countries are inherently different, (3) development can be administered, (4) developmental know-hows are transferable, and (5) the political, social, and cultural context of development can be easily altered.

Likewise, Fred Riggs, in his "Frontiers of Development," identified two foci in development administration: development of administration and the administration of development. Most development administration scholars focused more on the latter and it subsequently became synonymous to the administration of development in third world countries(Khator, 1998).

Given the situations above, DA maybe considered as "Management of Innovation" because it was aimed at helping countries that are undergoing reconstruction and social transformation.

Another school of thought emerged in response to the prescriptive theories which mainly prescribed numerous administrative principles, which led to the descriptive theories which focused on the describing the administrative decision-making processes.

Most of Herbert Simon's contribution to Public Administration was at a time when Scientific Management was fading away as a result of Bureaucratic Management antithesis and Human Relationists were campaigning for an employee friendly environment.

The main contribution of Herbert Simon to Public Administration was the process of decision making. Herbert agrees with Fayol and Weber before him that there is need for organizational structure. Unlike Fayol who saw the structure as an aid in ensuring work is efficiently done and Weber who had respect for structure in ensuring command, Herbert sees organization structure as an created for decision making.

He argues that decisions are made at all the levels of organization and not necessarily at the top and communicated downwards as Weber had argued. Every decision may affect less or more members within the organization and therefore there is need to pay attention to finer details of the decision for posterity.

Herbert thus contends that it is absolutely important to pay attention to values of the organization paying ethical and factual issues. As such every decision should be a mixture of facts as identified in the decision making process and the values of the organization.

Herbert Simon demonstrates that for every principle of organization management in literature, there existed counter-principles. Simon counterattacks the principles of organization management in the famous article called "The Proverbs of Administration," in which he pointed out the ambiguities and contradictions in the Gulick-Urwick principles stated a decade before.

Let's take an easy example. There is an old saying that knowledge is power, which is regarded as true. And there is another saying that ignorance is bliss, which is also reckoned as true. In that case, what should we do? Likewise some principles of organization management is contradictory.

Let's also look into Simon's examples. He disputed, contingent on the conditions, in order to defend one's choice of action or inaction in a specific situation, one might invoke the proverb "look before you leap" or "he who hesitates is lost."

For example, he perceived that both the span of control to limit the number of subordinates who directly report to certain managers and at the same time to lessen the number of an organization's hierarch were allowable but conflicting management principles.

Herbert Simon

In order to flatten the organizational pyramid, one must certainly increase a manager's span of control, which is the problem Simon established. Therefore, essentially puzzling are the two guiding principles. Simon referred to these principles as "proverbs of administration." Simon's ideas are that proverbs can't be used to demonstrate scientific theory.

TOEIC for Chapter 5.

01 Simon demonstrates that for every _____ of organization management in literature, there existed counter-principles.

(A) principle (B) principles (C) principals (D) principal

해설 every나 each는 단수 취급

Everybody is alright. Each one of you is OK.

따라서 답은 (A) principle

※ 다음 문제는 틀린 답을 선택하시오.

02 Another school of thought which _____ the role and problems of administration in developing countries calls its field Comparative Public Administration.

(A) started to study (B) started studying

(C) began study (D) began studying

03 Did you finish _____ ?

(A) to study (B) studying (C) at studying (D) in studying

해설 시작하다 start와 begin은 부정사와 동명사를 모두 사용할 수 있는 동사인 반면, finish는 동명사만을 목적어로 한다.

She started to sing a song. = She started singing a song.

따라서 2번 답은 (C) began study

따라서 3번 답은 (B) studying

04 I remember _____ you before.

(A) to meet (B) on meeting (C) for meeting (D) meeting

05 We must remember _____ the chairman tomorrow.

(A) meet (B) to meet (C) meetings (D) to have met

해설 부정사와 동명사로 썼을 때 의미가 다른 경우도 있다.

▸remember / forget 다음에 to Root가 오면 미래의 의미이고,
Root-ing가 오면 과거의 의미를 나타낸다.

따라서 4번 답은 (D) meeting
따라서 5번 답은 (B) to meet

06 We regret ______ that the plane bound for Guam will leave tow hours behind schedule.

(A) to say (B) on saying (C) for saying (D) saying

해설 ▸regret 다음에 to Root가 오면 ~하게 되어서 유감이다(미래의 의미), 그리고 Root-ing를 쓰면 ~한 것을 후회하다(과거의 의미)라고 번역을 한다.
따라서 답은 (A) to say

07 ______ development administration scholars focused more on the latter.

(A) The most (B) A most (C) Most (D) The most of

해설 the most는 최상급에 사용, 대부분의 ~라는 의미는 most
따라서 답은 (C) Most

Vocabulary for TOEIC

1. contribution
2. argue
3. flatten
4. reckon = consider = think of
5. perceive = recognize = see
6. span of control
7. contend = argue
8. pay attention to = attend to
9. identify = verify
10. proverb = old saying
11. resurrect = make alive again

References

Riggs, Fred W.(1957). Agraria and Industria. Toward a Typology of Comparative Administration. In: Siffin William J (ed.) *Toward the Comparative Study of Public Administration*. Indiana, USA: Bloomington.

______(1961). *The Ecology of Public Administration*. New Delhi, Bombay: Asia Publishing House.

______(1962). Trends in the Comparative Study of Public Administration. *International Review of Administrative Sciences*, 28(1): 9–15.

______(1964). *Administration in Developing Countries: The Theory of Prismatic Society*. Boston: Houghton Mifflin Co.

______(1970). The Idea of Development Administration. In: Edward Weidner (ed.) *Development Administration in Asia*. Durham, NC: Duke University Press, 25–72.

Simon, Herbert A.(1994). *Administrative Behavior; How Organizations can be Understood in Terms of Decision Making Process*. Roskide: Roskide University Press.

______(1947). *Administrative Behavior: A Study of Decision–Making Processes in Administrative Organization*, 4th ed., The Free Press.

Simon, Herbert A., & James G. March(1958). *Organizations*. New York: Wiley.

United Nations(1975). Development Administration: Current Approaches and Trends.

06
Chapter

Paradigm 4: PA as Management, 1950s~1970s

Your nation will succeed or fail to the degree that all of us citizens and businesses alike are active participants in building strong, sustainable and enriching communities.

—Arnold Hiatt, Former Ceo of the Stride rite Corp

LEARNING OBJECTIVES

After reading Chapter 6 in the textbook, the student should be able to:

1. Understand the management science.
2. Understand the three levels of government information systems.

Scientific management, bureaucracy and principles of management gave way to administrative management science. Management science is the application of statistical or mathematical methods and principles to business decision-making and problem-solving processes.

Applying scientific methods to common management situations can help governments and companies develop a deeper understanding of scenarios and how to approach these issues from a managerial standpoint.

Management science may also take a more theoretical approach to making decisions or solving problems rather than relying on a manager's personal judgment or perception of situations.

A relevant development in public administration is the emergence of management science and new technologies such as computers. In particular, computers have shown great promise for improving management and decision-making in public organizations. Various factors have contributed to the popularity of management science in public administration such as the growing complexity of public policy issues.

Some argue that the introduction of management science in public administration is an attempt to replace politics with science, and contend that science cannot solve social problems.

Others criticize the inadequacy of management science to deal with the complexities of social phenomena, and the likelihood of ignoring critical variables in the search for determinate solutions.

Specific techniques such as PPBS(Planning, Programming, Budgeting System) and cost-benefit analysis have also come under criticism for a variety of reasons, including their normative content and excessive market orientation.

The proper values in decision-making are compromise, consensus, negotiation and bargaining to cope with ambiguities and indeterminate issues. Finally, incrementalism is viewed as an appropriate response to political processes.

Management science, any application of science to the study of management. Originally a synonym for operations research, the term management science now designates a distinct field. Whereas operations research affords analytical data, statistics, and methods to increase the efficiency of management systems, management science applies these tools in such fields as big data, PMIS(Public Management Information System), data mining, engineering, economic forecasting, and logistics.

The use of information technology(IT) in public administration has been developed in two dimensions: office automation and information system. And IT made public administrators excited. The office automation seeks to raise efficiency and productivity of office business, and information system aims at organizing and utilizing information to support administration and management as well as policy development and decision-making, so as to improve effectiveness, efficiency, and productivity of an organization as a whole.

Office automation consists mainly of three components: word processing, data processing, and communications. Word processing technology includes word processors, electronic editors, xerox machines, scanners, printers, plotters, project panels, and desk-top publishing.

Capture devices (optical character recognition, digitizer) and mass storage support (magnetic, optical: CD-ROM, CD-R/W) are designed for accelerating data input and storage. Database and spreadsheet software are used for data processing and calculations in an office environment.

Multi-function telephones, facsimile machines, electronic mail, electronic conferencing, etc., are the tools provided by information technology to improve communications between offices.

In addition to the three aspects, some other applications of computer software, such as presentation, graphics, and various business software, are also extensively used to raise the efficiency and productivity of office business.

An information system is a mechanism used for acquiring, filing, storing, and retrieving an organized body of knowledge. Generally speaking, an information system is composed of computing hardware, software, and communication facilities. These are tangible portions of an information system.

The intangible portion of an information system, which is crucial and usually neglected, is the organizational aspects of an information system. User requirements analysis, data capturing and cleaning, data maintenance and updating, and information etc., all need to be well planned and organized.

Any information system, no matter how advanced its hardware and software are, cannot possibly be successful unless management and organizational aspects are a top concern.

The integration of the microcomputer and other electronic office facilities is becoming one of the main trends of office automation.

At the early stages of computer applications, computing power was largely concentrated in data processing(DP), such as the first computer payroll system, developed in 1954. Applications development was then directed towards support of management and decision-making organizations, i.e., so called management information systems(MIS) and decision-making support systems(DSS).

Before 1980s, people had been working on computerizing their business processes, i.e, using computers to automate or aid business activities as much as possible.

With the rapid development of information technology, particularly distributed processing and network computing, the concept of IT use in the public sector has changed dramatically. The focus of IT use, therefore, has shifted from the acquisition and implementation of computer equipment and systems to ensuring their optimal exploitation by means of adjustments to procedures, organization and staff utilization.

Accordingly, a shift in emphasis has taken place from efficiency and productivity gains by automating routine tasks, to achievement of effectiveness expressed in terms of applying new solutions to traditional tasks and providing solutions to new tasks.

The applications development of computers in organizations has been redirected from computerizing existing business processes of organizations to redesigning business processes and/or re-engineering organizations to take full advantage of and best benefit from information technology.

Many government agencies and enterprises in developed countries are quickly restructuring their organizations to make them computer-friendly and implementing more appropriate procedures compatible with an IT environment.

In the process, they are eliminating layers of traditional management, compressing job categories, creating work teams, training employees in multi-level skills, shortening and simplifying various business processes, and streamlining administration. The results have been impressive.

Three Levels of Government Information Systems

Government, like many other organizations, can be viewed as a three-level entity: strategic, managerial or administrative(tactical), and operational.

Each level represents a different level of control and has a different level of data requirement and view of the government.

The strategic level is the highest level either in a government organization or a government as a whole. This level is responsible for the sector's or entire government's policy and direction; it is primarily oriented toward functions rather than toward processes and tasks. Strategic data are highly concentrated and usually contain little detail.

The managerial or administrative level controls and organizes the actions of an organization. It also performs the supervisory activities aimed at ensuring correct input processing and monitors processing rates and quality.

The managerial level is responsible for the tactical implementation of the policies and directions received from the strategic level. It is oriented toward functions and processes. Managerial data are more fluid and limited than those of the operational level In most cases data at this level are extracted from operational reports. Managerial data needs are not as immediate as those of the operational level.

The operational level is data — and processing — oriented. Its inputs are specific and derived from current data events. It is the operational level which is the predominant recipient of data in the organization.

Figure 6–1 DIKW Pyramid

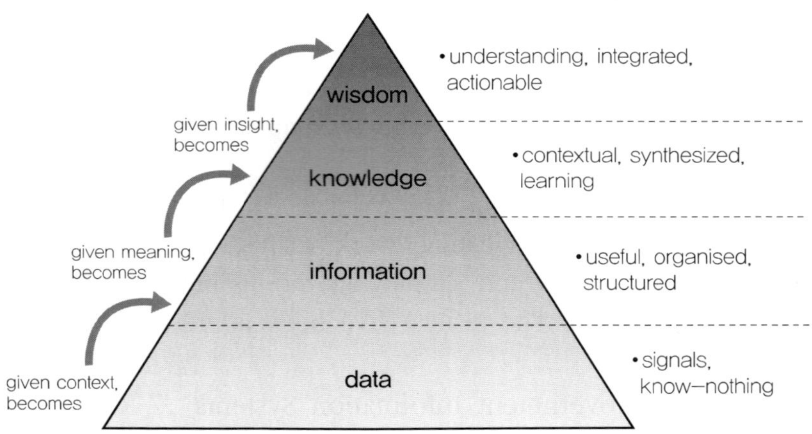

Source: https://sites.google.com/site/mattearspan/artifact-2

The operational level is primarily oriented toward processing and task, rather than toward functions. These operational areas are usually the first to be systematized and the first to be computerized. Their activities are particularly suited to systematization, and they are already subject to high degrees of standardization and normalization.

Corresponding to the three levels of government organizations, government information systems also can be divided into three different categories: (i) operational systems, (ii) management information systems, and (iii) decision-making support systems.

Operational Systems

Operational systems are the systems which support the people at the operational level. They are characterized as being transaction-based, cyclically processed, usually batch-oriented, and usually operating in a current time frame. That is, the transactions are accumulated and processed on a periodic basis. The files created from those transactions represent the accumulation period and are designed for expediency of processing rather than for the production of information.

Typical operational systems in a government are statistical data-processing systems in public sectors, accounting systems, payment-processing systems, revenue systems, customs systems, and the like.

Management Information Systems

Systems at this level are developed on a client-specific basis and are used to facilitate and control the day-to-day business of the organization. These systems are customized to the needs of the user client and are usually under the control of the user.

Management information systems are broader-based and more horizontal in nature, and they usually arise from the operational files of the ministry. There are applications within management information systems, but they are more on the order of reporting than processing.

Examples for management information systems in government are financial management information systems, personnel management information systems, programmes/projects management information systems, civil registration systems, enterprises registration systems, motor vehicle registration systems, passport management systems, patents management information systems, land management information systems, police information systems, judicial information systems, information systems for national defense and security, and information systems for various public sectors.

Decision–Making Support Systems

Emphasis in the use of decision support systems is on providing support to decision makers in terms of increasing the effectiveness of the decision–making effort. Generally, decision support systems are used for strategic and sometimes tactical situations.

The primary components of a decision support system are a database management system, a model–base management system, and a dialogue generation and management system. Obviously, decision support systems usually are built based on operational systems and management information systems existing within the organizations.

Examples of decision support systems in a Government are national, sectoral, and urban/regional planning information systems, natural resources information systems, laws and regulations information systems, scientific and technological information systems, social and economic information systems, demographic information systems, manpower information systems, executive information systems, and so forth. Artificial intelligence such as Alpha Go and expert systems have been developed rapidly as efficient tools to support and aid decision–making.

TOEIC for Chapter 6.

01 IT made public administrators _____.

(A) exciting (B) to excite (C) excite (D) excited

02 Her fantastic speech made the audience _____

(A) fascinating (B) to fascinate (C) fascinate (D) fascinated

Key Point

[TOEIC 시험에 등장하는 주요 사역동사] − S + let + O + O.C(5형식)
have

사역동사는 항상 5형식 문장에서만 사용이 된다.

사역동사 다음에 오는 목적어와 목적보어(서로 주어 + 동사의 관계임)가 능동의 관계이면 목적어 자리에 동사원형(Root)을 쓰고, 수동의 관계이면 과거분사(p.p.)를 쓴다.
He had the man (repair) my vehicle. 내가 시켰다. + 그 남자가 내 차를 고쳤다.
(능동)
▷ repair 5형식의 특징: 목적어와 목적보어 사이에 S + V 관계 성립
= He had his vehicle (repair) by the man. ▷ repaired로 바꿔야 함. (수동)

5형식 문형: S+V+O+O · C(불완전 타동사)

◇ S + V + O + 명사, 대명사: 목적어와 equal
형용사: 목적어의 상태 설명
부정사, 현재분사: 목적어와의 관계 능동적
과거분사: 목적어와의 관계 수동적

① O · C가 명사 또는 대명사
* He is a great scholar. (2형식)
= I believe him (to be) a great scholar. (5형식)

② 목적격 보어가 형용사일 때
* I believe him diligent.

③ 목적격 보어가 부정사

* I ordered him to go.
to stay in bed.
to take a rest.

사역동사:

I had my hair cut.
I had my picture taken.
I had my tooth pulled.
I let her go.
I made her fall in love with me.
I get her to go.

해설 사역동사 다음에 오는 목적어와 목적보어(서로 주어+동사의 관계임)가 능동의 관계이면 목적어 자리에 동사원형(Root)을 쓰고, 수동의 관계이면 과거분사(p.p.)를 쓴다.

따라서 1번 답은 (D) excited
따라서 2번 답은 (D) fascinated

03 _____ scientific methods to common management situations can help governments and companies develop a deeper understanding of scenarios.

(A) Application of
(B) Applying
(C) To be apply
(D) Applying of

Key Point

[부정사] – 형태는 To+동사원형(Root)이고 품사는 일정하게 정해져 있지 않다. 즉, 문장 상황에 따라 품사가 달라진다. 명사, 형용사, 부사 중 하나이다.

To study mathematics is hard. (명사)
She has a lot of reading materials to read. (형용사)
She is going abroad to study public administration. (부사)

[동명사] – 형태는 동사원형(Root)+ing이고 품사는 명사이다.

그렇다면, 부정사와 동명사는 어떤 관계가 있는가? 부정사가 문장에서 명사로 쓰일 때는 주어, 보어, 목적어 역할을 한다. 동명사도 역시 명사이므로 주어, 보어, 목적어로 사용된다. 따라서 부정사의 명사적 용법과 동명사는 원칙적으로 같다라는 결론에 도달할 수 있다.

Teaching is learning. = To teach is to learn.
She started to sing a song. = She started singing a song.

해설 (A) Application of는 정답으로 착각하기 쉬우나 of 이하로 한정되어 있어 앞에 The가 들어가야 한다.
따라서 답은 (B) Applying

※ 다음 중 틀린 것은?

04 Office automation _____ three components: word processing, data processing, and communications.

(A) is composed of (B) is made up of
(C) consists of (D) comprise from

해설 ~로 구성되다 be composed of = consist of = be made up of = comprise
(which is) composed of 관계대명사 주격과 be 동사는 생략 가능
따라서 답은 (D) comprise from

Vocabulary for TOEIC

1. replace = change
2. integration
3. in addition to
4. concentrate
5. eliminate = abolish = banish = get away with
6. shorten
7. streamline = rationalize
8. strategic
9. managerial
10. administrative
11. tactical
12. operational
13. predominant = prevailing = dominant
14. Alpha Go
15. expert system
16. artificial intelligence(AI)
17. regional

References

Simon, Herbert A.(1994). *Administrative Behavior; How Organizations can be Understood in Terms of Decision Making Process*. Roskide: Roskide University Press.

______(1947). *Administrative behavior: A Study of Decision-Making Processes in Administrative Organization*, 4th ed., The Free Press.

Simon, Herbert A., & James G. March(1947). *Organizations*. New York: Wiley.

United Nations(1951). *Standards and Techniques of Public Administration.*

______(1961). *Handbook of Public Administration: Current Concepts and Practices with Special References to Developing Countries.*

Chapter 07

Paradigm 5: PA as Public Administration, 1970s~1990s

Everything that lives, lives not alone, not for itself.

—William Blake, English Poet, Painter, and Printmaker

LEARNING OBJECTIVES

After reading Chapter 7 in the textbook, the student should be able to:

1. Understand the New Public Administration.
2. Understand the New Public Management(NPM) and Reinventing Government movement.
3. Compare the differences between traditional bureaucratic theory and NPM.
4. Understand the five strategies and approaches of government reinvention

New Public Administration(1970s)

The term "New Public Administration" or New PA may have emerged from the Minnowbrook Conference in 1968 in Syracuse University(Marini, 1971). The conference was the brainchild and inspiration of Dwight Waldo who brought together young public administrators and scholars to discuss important issues and varying perspectives on public administration.

One of its controversies is that it had rejected the classical theories of public administration and instead offered new principles. For instance, Frederickson in his essay, "Towards a New Public Administration," adds social equity to the classic definition of public administration. Conventional or classic public administration sought to only answer inquiries on efficiency and effectiveness like: how can the government offer better services with available resources (efficiency) or how can we maintain our level of services while spending less money (economy)? In introducing the principles of New PA, he adds the question: "Does this service enhance social equity?"

New Public Management and Reinventing Government(1980s to 1990s)

In the 1980s and early 1990s, as if there was a collective assault on the organization questioning conventional and traditional ways of doing things — both in the private and public sectors — various strategies and modalities underscoring the imperative for fundamental internal and external reform in the organization emerged. They ranged from being more "client" or "customer" oriented, to the decentralization of authority to being more "business oriented" especially for those in government.

The new public management(NPM) movement was apparently practiced by the European countries in the late 1907s and 1980s but was essentially launched several luminaries such as Christopher Hood(1991), Christopher Pollitt(1990), & Michael Barzeley(1992), among others in early 1990s. Similar movements such as reinventing government and reengineering also emerged around the same time. This section introduces NPM, reinventing government and reengineering government. When did these ideas emerge? What were their key features? And were these really more of the same?

The New Public Management(NPM) movement has started in the late 1970s in UK under the Thatcher government; however aside from England, NPM has also long been practiced by the other members of the Organization for Economic Cooperation and Development(OECD) mostly Anglo－Saxon countries like New Zealand, Australia, Germany, the Netherlands, and Canada in the 1980s.

The best example of the NPM practice can be seen in New Zealand's administrative reforms. Their government privatized substantial public functions, redeveloped their personnel system in order to be more performance－oriented, instituted new processes of productivity measures, and reengineered departmental systems to reflect government's commitment(Boston, 1996; as cited in Denhardt, 2004: 136－137).

In the US, during the administration of US President Bill Clinton and Vice President Al Gore, this concept was reflected in their "National Performance Review" which has urged the federal government to improve its performance. This has also led the foundation of the praxis of reengineering government led by the Clinton－Gore administration.

Moreover, NPM is a shift into a managerialist movement, identifying five core beliefs of managerialism: (1) the main route to social progress lies in the achievement of continuing increases in economically defined productivity; (2) such productivity increase will mainly come from the application of ever more sophisticated technologies; (3) the application of these technologies can only be achieved with a labor force disciplined in accordance with the productivity ideal; (4) management is a separate and distinct organizational function and one that plays the crucial role in planning, implementing and measuring the necessary improvements in productivity; and (5) to perform this crucial role, managers must be granted reasonable "room to maneuver"(i.e. right to manage")(Pollitt, 1990: 2－3; as cited in Denhardt, 2000: 148).

The ideas of "new public management" and "reinventing government" were essentially born out of the continuing search for solutions to economic problems in 1970s and to produce a government that "works better but costs less"(Denhart, 2004: 136).

The idea of "reinventing government" was advanced by Osborne and Gaebler in 1992. Their concept Their concept of NPM was sparked by the use of business model prescriptions for government i.e. using private sector innovation, resources, and organizational ideas to improve the public sector. Reinventing Government provided ten principles through which public entrepreneurs might bring about massive governmental reform principles that has remained at the core of the new public management.

Osborne & Gaebler(1992) criticizes the bureaucratic government which was efficient in the industrial society and argues that in this information era the following ten commandments are should be emphasized.

1. Steer more than they row.
2. Empower communities rather than simply delivering services.
3. Encourage competition rather than monopoly.
4. Are driven by their missions, not their rules.
5. Fund outcomes rather than inputs.
6. Meet customer needs, not bureaucracy's.
7. Concentrate on earning, not just spending.
8. Invest in prevention rather than cure.
9. Decentralize authority.
10. Solve problems by leveraging the marketplace, rather than simply creating public programs.

Table 7–1 Osborne and Gaebler's Principles of NPM

Government	Traditional Bureaucracy	New Public Management
Catalytic government	rowing	steering
Community–owned	serving	empowering
Competitive	monopolistic service delivery	competitive service delivery
Mission–driven	rule–driven	Mission–driven
Results–oriented	inputs	outcomes
Customer–driven	bureaucracy	customer
Enterprising	spending	earning
Anticipatory	cure	prevention
Decentralized	hierarchy, control	participation, teamwork
Market–oriented	administrative–oriented	market–oriented

Source: Osborne, David & Ted Gaebler(1992), *Reinventing Government: How the Entrepreneurial Spirit is Transforming the Public Sector.*

In Banishing Bureaucracy, David Osborne teams with Peter Plastrik to further explore the process of making public and governmental organizations more entrepreneurial by introducing businesslike practices. The authors focus on five strategies for fundamentally changing the way government works on local, state, regional and national levels, and give plenty of real-life global success stories.

Implementation is to occur through five common-sense strategies: Clarify purposes (core), create incentives for employee performance (consequences), obtain feedback from service recipients (customer), empower people to do what is needed (control), and replace old habits with new commitments (culture).

And they provide numerous examples that introduce some substance into the discussion, and from Indianapolis city government to Minnesota schools, the US Forest Service, and national government in New Zealand.

There are many ways to categorize these fundamental levers of change.

We have grouped them into five basic strategies, each of which includes several distinct approaches and many tools. For each lever, we have designated a strategy. And to help people remember the strategies, we have given each one a label that begins with the letter C.

The Core Strategy

The first critical piece of DNA determines the purpose of public systems and organizations. If an organization is unclear about its purpose—or has been given multiple and conflicting purposes—it cannot achieve high performance.

The Consequences Strategy

The second key piece of DNA determines the incentives built into public systems. Bureaucratic DNA gives employees powerful incentives to follow the rules and keep their heads down. Innovation can only bring trouble; the status quo brings steady rewards. Employees are paid the same regardless of the results they produce.

The Customer Strategy

The next fundamental piece of system DNA focuses primarily on accountability, specifically, to whom are the organizations accountable? To be precise, all five strategies touch on the issue of accountability. The core strategy defines what an organization is accountable for; the consequences strategy determines how it will be held accountable; the control strategy affects who will be accountable; and the culture strategy helps employees internalize their accountability. But by making organizations accountable to their customers, the customer strategy deals most powerfully with the issue of accountability.

Most public entities are accountable to elected officials, who create them, determine their functions, and fund them. Because these officials are under constant pressure to respond to the demands of interest groups, they often care more about where public resources are spent than about the results they purchase.

The Control Strategy

The fourth critical chunk of DNA determines where decision-making power lies. In bureaucratic systems, most of the power remains near the top of the hierarchy. In democracies, power first flows from citizens to elected officials; then from elected officials to central "staff" agencies such as budget and personnel offices; finally from those central control agencies down to agency line managers. Typically, elected officials keep as much power as possible in their own hands, and the central control agencies guard their power even more jealously. Line managers find their options limited and their flexibility constrained by detailed budget instructions, personnel rules, procurement systems, auditing practices, and the like. Their employees have almost no power to make decisions. As a result, government organizations respond to new orders rather than to changing situations or customers' needs.

The Culture Strategy

Finally, the last critical piece of DNA determines the culture of public organizations: the values, norms, attitudes, and expectations of employees. Bureaucratic systems use detailed specifications — functional units, procedural rules, and job descriptions — to mold what employees do.

They make initiative risky. As employees become habituated to these conditions, they become carriers of the culture. They become reactive, dependent, fearful of taking too much initiative themselves. In this way, bureaucratic DNA creates cultures of fear, blame, and defensiveness.

Reinventors use three approaches to reshape the culture; they mold the organization's habits, hearts, and minds. They develop new habits by giving people new experiences — new kinds of work and interactions with new people.

They reinforce these new behaviors by helping people shift their emotional commitments: their hopes, fears, and dreams. And they support this new emotional covenant by building a shared vision of the future, a new mental model of where the organization is going and how it will get there.

Some of you may be saying to yourselves, "This all sounds logical, but it will never work here. My city (or county, or province, or country) is different."

Your government may not be ready to reinvent, but when it is, rest assured, these strategies will apply. They work in small cities and large nations, in parliamentary systems and presidential systems, in strong mayor cities and council manager cities.

Different kinds of organizations require different approaches as well.

There are four basic types of public organizations: policy, regulatory, service, and compliance. Service organizations deliver services. Policy organizations make policy decisions. Regulatory organizations set rules, and compliance organizations enforce them.

These distinctions are important, because reinventors who work at the organization level must apply the five strategies differently in different types of organizations. This can be tricky, since many organizations perform a mix of functions. Often they combine policy and service functions, or regulatory and compliance functions. Many service organizations, from schools to public housing developments, must also win compliance with standards of behavior.

Police departments are compliance organizations, but they perform services as well: guiding traffic around construction sites; performing crowd control at concerts; running youth sports programs. Many social benefit agencies, such as employment services and welfare offices, deliver services, write regulations, and enforce compliance with their rules.

Tax collection agencies are in the compliance business, but they typically offer services such as information hot lines. And many policy advice organizations are actually service rather than policy organizations, because they provide services to policy makers, rather than making policy decisions themselves.

Table 7-2 Government Organization Types and Examples

A Typology of Government Organizations	
Organization Type	*Example*
Policy	Planning Office; School Board
Regulatory	Federal Communications Commission Securities and Exchange Commission
Service Delivery External Customers	Public Works Department School District
Internal Customers	Data Processing Office Maintenance Department
Compliance External Compilers	Police Department; Occupational Safety and Health Administration
Internal Compilers	Auditors; Inspectors General

The five strategies play out quite differently in policy and compliance organizations than they do in service organizations. In compliance agencies, for instance, the customer strategy is more complex. These agencies' primary customers are the public at large, represented by elected executives and legislators.

But compliers—taxpayers, drivers, polluters—are also important. Then there are non-compliers: people and organizations that break the law, don't pay the taxes they owe, or ignore environmental regulations. Compliance organizations have to pay attention to all three categories.

Because some compliance organizations, such as the police and courts, are normally required to treat every complier the same—or at least to treat similar classes of compliers equally—there are limits to how much flexibility they can allow their employees.

If you want a qualitatively different kind of public system or organization, you must rewrite the genetic code. You can generate a series of innovations without using the five C's, but you cannot create a continuously improving, selfrenewing system. Consider this the first rule of reinvention: No new DNA, no transformation(David Osborne & Peter Plastrik, 1997, *Banishing Bureaucracy: The Five Strategies for Reinventing Government*).

Table 7–3 The Five Strategies and Approaches of Government Reinvention

The Five C's		
Lever	*Strategy*	*Approaches*
Purpose	The Core Strategy	Strategic Management Clearing the Decks Uncoupling
Incentives	The Consequences Strategy	Managed Competition Enterprise Management Performance Management
Accountability	The Customer Strategy	Customer Choice Competitive Choice Customer Quality Assurance
Power	The Control Strategy	Organizational Empowerment Employee Empowerment Community Empowerment
Culture	The Culture Strategy	Changing Habits Touching Habits Winning Minds

Source: David Osborne & Peter Plastrik(1997). *Banishing Bureaucracy: The Five Strategies for Reinventing Government.*

TOEIC for Chapter 7.

01 NPM is a shift into a managerialist movement, ______ five core beliefs of managerialism.

(A) identifyed (B) it identified (C) it identifys (D) identifying

Key Point

분사구문의 종류

① 시간(~할 때)

* Walking along the street, she met an old friend of mine.
=While she walked along the street, she met an old friend of mine.

* Left alone, I began to read.
=When I was left alone, I began to read.

② 이유, 원인(~이므로)

* Not knowing what to do, I asked for her advice. (부정어는 분사 앞에)
=As I didn't know what to do, I asked for her advice.

* Tired, I went to bed early.
=As I was tired, I went to bed early.

③ 조건(~한다면)

* Turning to the left, you will find the house.
=If you turn to the left, you will find the house.

* Some books, read carelessly, will do more harm than good.
=Some books, if they are read carelessly, will do more ~

④ 양보(비록 ~한다 할지라도)

* Admitting what you say, I still don't believe it.
=Though I admit what you say, I still don't believe it.

* Born of the same parents, they bear no resemblance to each other.
=Though they were born of the same parents, they bear ~

⑤ 부대상황(동시동작: while, as; ~하면서)

* Smiling brightly, she extended her hand.
=While she smiled brightly, she extended her hand.

* Walking on tiptoe, I approached the window.
=I walked on tiptoe and approached the window.

* Singing and dancing together, we had a good time.
=As we sang and danced together, we had a good time.
with+목적어+분사(부대상황) ⇒ 생생한 묘사적 효과
* He sat silently, and the cat was dozing at his feet.

해설 따라서 답은 (D) identifying

02 In _____ Bureaucracy, David Osborne further explores the process of making governmental organizations more entrepreneurial.

(A) Banished (B) Banishing (C) Banishing (D) Banishing in

03 Not too many years ago, it was an _______ experience to travel 70 miles from hometown.

(A) excited (B) excite (C) exciting (D) excitedly

Key Point

[분사] - 현재분사: 동사원형(Root)+-ing: 능동, 진행을 의미한다.
과거분사: 동사원형(Root)+-ed(p.p.): 수동, 완료를 뜻한다.
품사는 형용사이다(명사를 수식하거나, 보어로 쓰인다).

TOEIC에서는 대개 부정사와 동명사가 결부된 문제가 출제되고(목적어로 무엇을 쓰는가 하는 것 등) 분사는 따로 출제된다. 즉, 분사의 수식을 받는 명사와 분사 사이의 관계(분사가 명사를 수식하는 경우), 또는 분사의 의미상의 주어와 분사의 관계(분사가 보어로 쓰일 경우)가 **능동일 때는 현재 분사를, 수동일 때는 과거 분사**를 쓰는 문제가 출제된다.

분사 문제에 자주 등장하는 동사는 타동사들이다.

▸ 예: surprise(놀라게 하다), excite(흥분시키다), interest(관심 있게 하다), satisfy(만족시키다), embarrass(당황하게 하다), depress(풀죽게 하다), disappoint(실망시키다), please(기쁘게 하다), discourage(낙심시키다), frighten(두려워하게 하다), frustrate(좌절시키다), fascinate(매혹시키다), locate(위치시키다, 찾다), bore(싫증나게 하다)

▸ 위의 단어들은 분사 문제에 가장 많이 등장하는 타동사들이므로 반드시 암기해야 한다.

해설 현재분사는 능동, 진행을 의미하므로 exciting experience가 맞다. 경험이 수동적으로 흥분당할 수 없다.
흥분을 야기하는 경험
excited experience는 흥분된 경험이라는 의미로 수동을 뜻해 경험이 흥분할 수 없어 논리적으로 맞지 않음.

banish의 경우도 마찬가지이다.
따라서 2번 답은 (B) Banishing
따라서 3번 답은 (C) exciting

Vocabulary for TOEIC

1. emerge
2. social equity
3. enhance = improve
4. external
5. underscore = underline = emphasize
6. praxis = application and practice of theory
7. reengineer = redesign
8. in accordance with
9. Steer
10. catalytic
11. occur = take place = happen
12. strategy
13. critical = vital = significant = important
14. accountable = responsible
15. procurement = purchase = buying
16. shift = change
17. clear thew decks = preparation for action, event or war
18. uncouple = separate = divide
19. touch = move = impress
20. compliance = obedience

References

Frederickson, George H., & Kevin B. Smith(2003). *The Public Administration Theory Primer.* Westview Press.

Marini, Frank(1971). *Toward a New Public Administration.* The Minnowbrook Perspective. Chandler Publishing Company.

Osborne, David & Peter Plastrik(1997). *Banishing Bureaucracy: The Five Strategies for Reinventing Government.* Perseus Books.

Osborne, David & Ted Gaebler(1992). *Reinventing Government: How the Entrepreneurial Spirit is Transforming the Public Sector.* Penguin Books.

08 Chapter

Paradigm 6: From Government to Governance, 1990s~

LEARNING OBJECTIVES

After reading Chapter 8 in the textbook, the student should be able to:

1. Understand the concept of governance.
2. Understand the components or indicators of governance.

Governance can be traced back to the Greek verb "kubernan"(to pilot or steer) and was used by Plato to design a system or rule. World Bank defines Governance is the institutional capacity of public organizations to provide the public and other goods demanded by a country's citizens or their representatives in an effective, impartial, and accountable manner subject to resource constraints.

1. PA as Governance(1990s into the 2000)

The many failed development interventions in the 1950s into the 1990s spurred the introduction of other development reforms. The "governance" paradigm was introduced and advocated by the United Nations(UN), World Bank(WB), Asian Development Bank(ADB) and other international institutions.

The word "governance" suddenly "has become something of a mantra in recent years, uttered by donors, reformers and specialists alike"(Frechette, 2000: 25).

Governance entails a larger scope and has a wider meaning. Though the term "governance" has been used to refer mostly to "government," when correctly used, "governance" really goes beyond government. It involves the institutionalization of a system through which citizens, institutions, organizations, and groups in a society articulate their interests, exercise their rights, and mediate their differences in pursuit of the collective good(ADB, 1995; as cited in ADB, 2005: 1). And it also has various levels.

Figure 8-1 The Levels of Governance

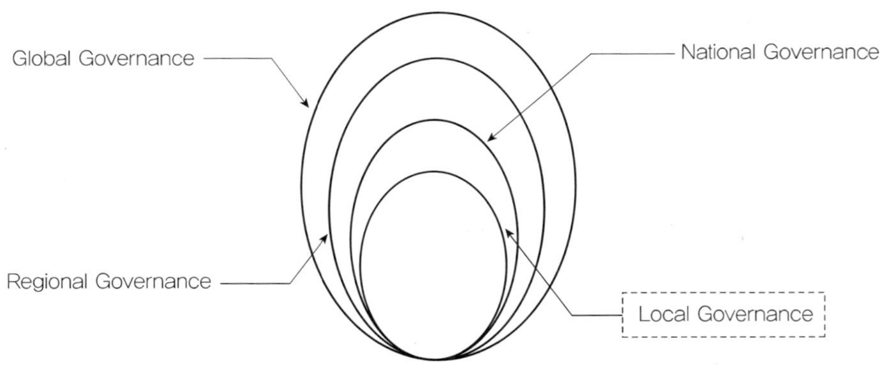

UNDP describes it as "the exercise of political, economic and administrative authority to manage a nation's affairs. It embraces all of the methods — good and bad — that societies use to distribute power and manage public resources and problems"(UNDP, 1997: 9).

Cariño(2000), in her reflections on the term "governance," identified actors and factors that pushed for governance. She acknowledges that governance is not the sole responsibility of the government per se but the role of the market and civil society are of equal importance too and should also be recognized.

She then identified the factors or processes that pushed for governance and some of these are: the quest for growth and development, the environmental movement, globalization and consolidating peace. These are practically the same values or virtues found in the UN Charter. Likewise, governance promotes the virtues of decentralization, participation, responsiveness and accountability among others.

The concept of "good governance" has emerged and became prominent in international aid circles around 1989 or 1990. It served as a general guiding principle for donor agencies to demand that recipient governments adhere to proper administrative processes in the handling of development assistance and put in place effective policy instruments towards that end handling of development assistance and put in place effective policy instruments towards that end(Doornbos, 2003). When there is good governance, there is sustainable development.

1. Accountability means making public officials answerable for government behavior and responsive to the entity from which they derive authority.

Accountability is a key requirement of good governance. Not only government institutions but also the private sector and civil society organizations must be accountable to the public and to their institutional stakeholders. Who is accountable to whom varies, depending on whether decisions or actions taken are internal or external to an organization or institution. In general, an organization or an institution is accountable to those who will be affected by its decisions or actions. Accountability cannot be enforced without transparency and the rule of law.

2. Participation refers to enhancing people's access to and influence on

public policy processes undertaking development for and by the people. In other words, participation means every man and woman must have their own voices heard in the policy determining process, directly or through a legitimate medium.

Participation by both men and women is a cornerstone of good governance. Participation could be either direct or through legitimate intermediate institutions or representatives. Representative democracy does not necessarily mean that the concerns of the most vulnerable in society would be taken into consideration in decision-making. Participation needs to be informed and organized, which requires freedom of association and expression and an organized civil society. The Eight Characteristics of Good Governance as Defined by the United Nations.

3. Transparency refers to the availability of Information to the general public and clear government rules, regulations, and decisions.

Transparency means that decisions made and their enforcement are achieved in a manner that follows rules and regulations. It also means that information is freely available and directly accessible to those who will be affected by such decisions and their enforcement. It also means that enough information is provided and that it is provided in easily understandable forms and media.

4. Effectiveness and Efficiency

Good governance means that processes and institutions produce results that meet the needs of society while making the best use of the resources at their disposal. The concept of efficiency in the context of good governance also covers the sustainable use of natural resources and the protection of the environment.

A society's well being depends on ensuring that all its members feel that they have a stake in it and do not feel excluded from the mainstream of society. This requires that all groups, but particularly the most vulnerable, have opportunities to improve or maintain their well being.

5. Responsiveness

Good governance requires that institutions and processes try to serve all stakeholders or share holders within a reasonable timeframe, respond actively to the needs of the public.

6. Rule of Law

Rule of law requires fair legal frameworks that are enforced impartially. It also requires full protection of human rights particularly those of minorities. It also reflects how well the legal and systematic apparatus is working. Impartial enforcement of laws requires an independent judiciary and an impartial and incorruptible police force.

TOEIC for Chapter 8.

01 Governance entails a _____ scope and has a wider meaning.

(A) larger　　(B) enlarge
(C) enlargement　　(D) largely

02 They are advertising luxury apartments ideal for the _____ young executive.

(A) successive　　(B) succession
(C) successful　　(D) success

Key Point

형용사는 명사를 수식하고, 부사는 1) 동사, 2) 형용사, 그리고 3) 다른 부사를 수식한다. scope가 명사이므로 형용사 large나 large의 비교급 형용사와 부사를 제대로 사용할 수 있는지를 묻는 문제들이 출제된다.

형용사
She is beautiful. = She is a beautiful girl.

부사
1. 부사의 형태
① 부사: 형용사+ly
* 형용사+ly: slow → slowly
careful → carefully
* −y+ly=ily−happy → happily
* le+ly=ly−possible → possibly
◇ 예외: sole → solely
whole → wholly
She walks beautifully. = She walks in beauty.

해설 따라서 1번의 답은 (A) larger
successive는 계승하는
따라서 2번 답은 (C) successful

03 She ______ that governance is not the sole responsibility of the government per se but the role of the market and civil society are of equal importance too and should also be recognized.

(A) acknowledge (B) acknowledges

(C) acknowledging (D) acknowledged

해설 3인칭 단수 현재

따라서 3번 답은 (B) acknowledges

Vocabulary for TOEIC

1. impartial = fair = just
2. advocate = support = stand by
3. refer to = consult = mention
4. articulate = express = show
5. per se = itself
6. recognize = know
7. acknowledge = admit
8. involve = include
9. efficiency = output/input
10. effectiveness = benefit/cost
11. sustainable = renewable
12. prominent = distinguished = outstanding = striking = noticeable
13. decentralization
14. handle = deal with = treat
15. derive = obtain = draw = get
16. stakeholder = shareholder = stockholder
17. enforce = enact = implement

References

Kaufmann, Daniel, Aart Kraay, & Pablo Zoido－Lobaton(2002). "Governance Matters Ⅱ: Updated Indicators for 2000－01." *Policy Research Working Paper 2772.* Washington: World Bank.

Keane, J.(1998). *Civil Society: Old Images, New Visions.* Stanford, CA: Stanford University Press.

Kettl, D.(1993). *Sharing Power: Public Governance and Private Markets.* Washington D.C.: Bookings Institution.

Peters, B. G.(1998). *The Future of Governing: Four Emerging Models.* Lawrence, Kansas: University Press of Kansas.

Rhodes, R.(2000). The Governance Narrative: Key Findings and Lessons from the ESRC's Whitehall Programme. *Public Administration,* 78(2): 345－363.

UNDP(1997). Developing Capacity for Effective Governance. A Workshop For UNDP.

09 Chapter

Approaches to PA

The government, which was designed for the people, has got into the hands of the bosses and their employers, the special interests. An invisible empire has been set up above the forms of democracy.

— Woodrow Wilson

LEARNING OBJECTIVES

After reading Chapter 3 in the textbook, the student should be able to:

1. Understand the various theories and approaches to public administration such as systems theory.
2. Understand the ecological approach.
3. Understand the behavioral approach.
4. Understand the public choice theory.
5. Understand the government failure and market failure.

1. Systems Theory

Systems theory is the interdisciplinary study of systems in general. And it can be applied to all types of systems at all levels in all fields of research. The term does not yet have a well-established, precise meaning, but systems theory can reasonably be considered a specialization of systems thinking, a generalization of systems science, a systems approach. The term originates from Bertalanffy's General System Theory(GST) and is used in later efforts in other fields, such as the action theory of Talcott Parsons and the systems-theory of Luhmann.

In this context the word systems is used to refer specifically to self-regulating systems, i.e. that are self-correcting through feedback. Self-regulating systems are found in nature, including the physiological systems of our body, in local and global ecosystems, and in climate—and in human learning processes.

An applications of System Theories is Complex Adaptive Systems(CAS). Complex adaptive systems are special cases of complex systems. They are complex in that they are diverse and made up of multiple interconnected elements and adaptive in that they have the capacity to change and learn from experience.

The term complex adaptive systems was coined at the interdisciplinary Santa Fe Institute(SFI), by John H. Holland, Murray Gell-Mann and others. However, the approach of the complex adaptive systems does not take into account the adoption of information which enables people to use it.

CAS ideas and models are essentially evolutionary. Accordingly, the theory of complex adaptive systems bridges developments of the system theory with the ideas of 'generalized Darwinism,' which suggests that Darwinian principles of evolution help explain a wide range of phenomena. In Part 2 organization theory, organization as CAS will be discussed in detail.

Herbert Simon once said that diagrams are worth a thousand words. The following figure depicts the diagram of the systems theory combining several scholars such as Easton, Almond, Riggs, Churchman.

Figure 9-1 Diagram of the Systems Theory

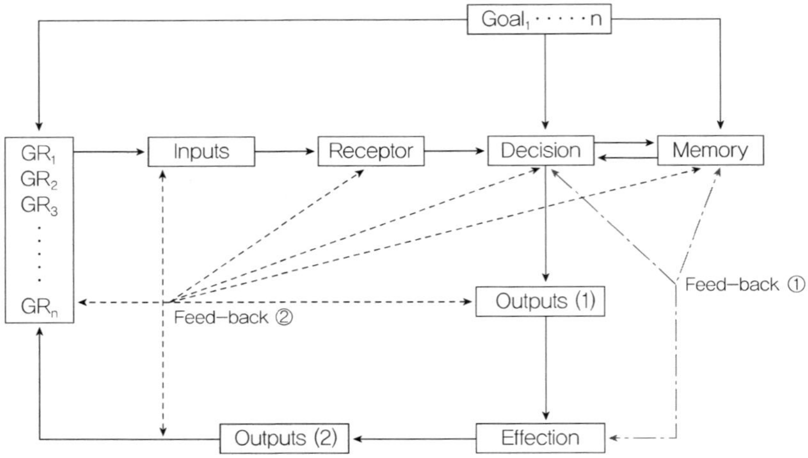

1. GR_i: Interest Groups increasing according to the level of diversification of social system.
2. Inputs: Maintenance Inputs that sustain system such as the demand of individuals groups, and media and Production Inputs which are processed to yield a productive outcome.
3. Receptor: The executive branch, the legislative branch, the judiciary.
4. Decision: Agencies that produce policy, program, project based on the objective and inputs.
5. Memory: Staff for effective policy-making.
6. Outputs: Outputs 1 is made up of policy, program, project, and laws Outputs 2 consists of the consequent outcomes of policy, program, project, and laws.
7. Effector: Implementing apparatus and processes that bring the outcomes of the outputs.
8. Goal: Goals of administrative and political system.
9. Feed-back:

9-1: Feedback as action monitor is comprised of that of groups which criticize or complain about the outputs and policy-making such as mass media and the opposite party.

9-2: Feedback as error detector includes an apparatus that inspects and audit elements within a system such as NIS and Board of Audit and

Inspection.

10. Entropy: The degree of disorder or uncertainty in a system Thus in open social system negentropy is used instead. Negentropy is reverse entropy. It means things becoming more in order. By 'order' is meant organisation, structure and function: the opposite of randomness or chaos.
11. Homeostasis: The property of a system, which keeps it balanced, stable, or not subject to change.
12. Equifinality: The principle that in open systems a given end state can be reached by many potential means. In other words, In the system there are many different ways of achieving the desired state of the system.

2. Ecological Approach

The ecological approach is much less abstract than systems theory, but has employed many of the concepts associated with it. Applying the ecological perspective in practice settings is helpful in determining the areas of greatest concern to public administration.

Ecology in public administration was primarily introduced by Professor John M. Gaus, one of the early pioneers of public administration. He emphasized that the public administration including its development as well as its activities were influenced by its setting or ecology.

Gaus have enumerated several ecological factors which he perceives to be affecting the manner in which the government responds to the changes in its general environment. These are people, place, physical technology, social technology, wishes and ideas, catastrophe, and personality. The interplay of these seven ecological factors to the dynamics of an administrative system in the government aids in explaining its past actions, as well as in predicting and determining possible courses of action in the future.

Not only private organizations but also public organizations within the environment are affected by the larger environments. PESTLE analysis is a framework used to scan the organizations external macro environment. PESTLE stands for Political, Economic, Social, Technological, Legal, and Environmental environments.

Figure 9–2 PESTLE Analysis

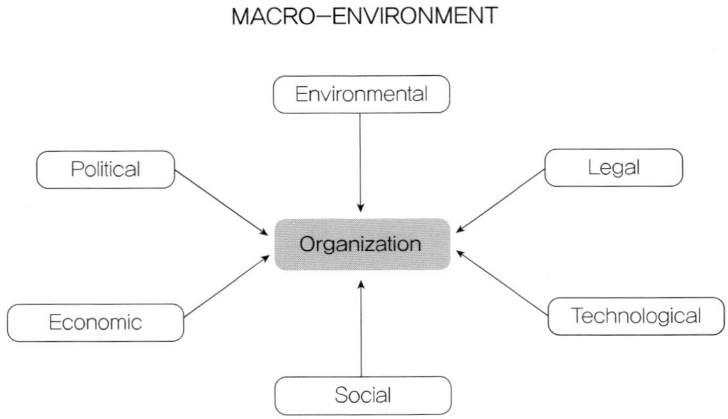

PESTLE analysis, Factsheets, CIPD.
Source: http://www.cipd.co.uk/hr-resources/factsheets/pestle-analysis.aspx [Accessed 18 Jul. 2016].

Riggs made a great effort in searching for an objective and effective model for analyzing public administration in developing regions. Riggs' most significant contribution was to create the administration model — the fused–prismatic–diffracted model. The model covers a wide range of research, for instance, economic life, social structures, political symbols, and the allocation of power are all part of the analysis of structural function. Moreover, the model can be applied in modern, traditional, developing and semi–developed economies. Riggs has consistently put a particular emphasis on the linkage between public administration and its environment, and therefore advocated the concept that the administrative behavior in a given society must be understood in the context of the social background instead of the administration itself.

He has constructed two models of societies. One is to represent modern industrial society and the other for agricultural societies. First one is called Industria. The next is agraria.

These are two polar types one representing contemporary America and imperial China is agraria respectively. He also identified a third category called transitia. Later he developed the prismatic model.

Riggs presented the concept of "prismatic society" to explain the unique conditions and the dynamics of politics and administration in developing countries.

He categorized societies into three

1. Fused, 2. Prismatic, 3. Diffracted.

He used Fused model to explain the ecology of traditional societies.

Prismatic society to explain the developing world.

Diffracted society to explain the developed societies.

As an alternative model for conceptualizing developing countries Riggs offered his "prismatic model" based on the metaphor of a prism. When white light (that is light made up of all visible wavelengths) passes through a prism it is diffracted broken into a variety of colors — a rainbow. Similarly Riggs contended societies in the process of development move from a fused mode in which little or no differentiation exists to a diffracted condition in which there is a high degree of functional specialization.

In administrative terms, this means a change from a situation in which a few structures perform a variety of functions, as in very underdeveloped conditions, to one in which many specific structures perform specific functions, as in highly developed societies like the industrial countries of the west.

Figure 9–3 Prismatic Model

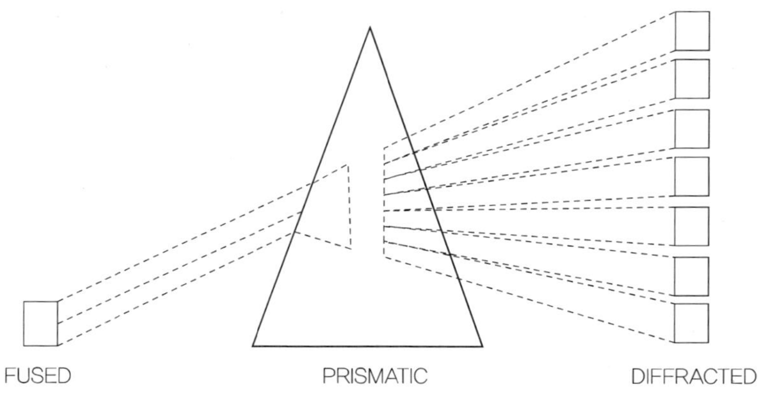

Riggs is often criticized for tearing down rather than building up, and for having nothing to offer to the understanding of administrative process except building new jargons.

Another critique of the "fused–prismatic–diffracted" model argues that while it is predicated on the notion of deduction, there is little empirical evidence to support it. Most sciences require empirical evidence so that results can be verified, not only repeatedly but also at any time and place. Moreover, objective comparisons would then likewise be possible. Riggs, however, endeavors to prescribe "formalism" as a given standard, and most scholars consider this concept as unsatisfactory. Moreover, when scholars attempt to use Riggs' model to study the administrative systems of foreign countries, they often encounter numerous difficulties.

T. Parsons once said that sociologists all critique Max Weber, but no one can do social research independently and scientifically without referring to Weber's theories. By the same token, those who study Comparative Public Administration will inevitably find reason to critique Fred W. Riggs' "fused prismatic diffracted model," but in conducting research, no one is free of Riggs' influence.

Recently the concept of ecological system is applied to that of C-P-N-D(Contents-Platform-Network-Device) ecological system. This notion can offer policy suggestions for the establishment of a new creative contents industry ecological system. Contents, platform, network, and device is inter-connected as if they constituted an ecological system.

Figure 9-4 C-P-N-D(Contents-Platform-Network-Device) Ecological System

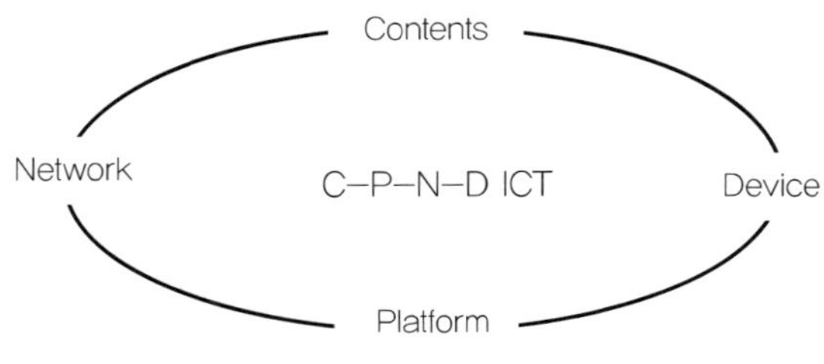

We can illustrate Psy's Music Video(MV) Gangnam Style as a case of C-P-N-D ecological system. In this ecological system, Psy's MV Gangnam Style is a good example of contents. YG Entertainment Group uploaded this MV on such platform as Youtube, spreading out widely all over the world through network such as internet. And finally world record viewers watch this famous MV using various devices like PC and smartphones.

Figure 9–5 C–P–N–D Case: Psy's MV Gangnam Style

3. Behavioral Approach

Behavioralism is an approach in public administration and political science which seeks to provide an objective, value–neutral, and quantified approach to explaining and predicting public administration and political behavior. It is associated with the rise of the behavioral sciences, modeled after the natural sciences.

To understand public administration and political behavior, behavioralism which distinguishes the fact from the value uses the following methods: sampling, interviewing, scoring and scaling and statistical analysis.

The theory of management can be traced back to the times of the pyramids in Egypt. As time went by, different ideals and perspectives about management emerged. One of the most notable was during the 1950s, when a man named Herbert Simon laid the foundation for a management theory based on a psychological perspective: The Behavioral Decision making theory. In short, the theory emphasized that, managers don't have all the information on all possible consequences and alternatives, created from their decisions.

From this perspective, this theory can be applied to any professional setting. The fact is every manager, in every company has to go through this cognitive limitation process, when it comes to decision making, which makes this theory applicable and true in its terms.

Contrary to the tenets of classical economics, Simon maintained that individuals do not seek to maximize their benefit from a particular course of action (since they cannot assimilate and digest all the information that would be needed to do such a thing). Not only can they not get access to all the information required, but even if they could, their minds would be unable to process it properly. The human mind necessarily restricts itself. It is, as Simon put it, bounded by "cognitive limits."

Hence people, in many different situations, seek something that is "good enough," something that is satisfactory. Humans, for example, when in shopping mode, aspire to something that they find acceptable, although that may not necessarily be optimal. They look through things in sequence and when they come across an item that meets their aspiration level they go for it. This real－world behaviour is what Simon called satisficing.

He applied the idea to organizations as well as to individuals. Managers do much the same thing as shoppers in a mall. "Whereas economic man maximizes, selects the best alternative from among all those available to him," he wrote, "his cousin, administrative man, satisfices, looks for a course of action that is satisfactory or 'good enough.'"

4. Public Choice Theory

Public choice or public choice theory refers to "the use of economic tools to deal with traditional problems of political science." James M. Buchanan & Gordon Tullock coauthored The Calculus of Consent: Logical Foundations of Constitutional Democracy(1962), considered one of the landmarks in public choice.

In particular, the preface describes the book as "about the political organization" of a free society. But its methodology, conceptual apparatus, and analytics "are derived, essentially, from the discipline that has as its subject the economic organization of such a society."

Public choice theory suggests that if public officials monopolize service delivery, then the result is oversupply and inefficiency(Blais & Dion, 1992; Jackson, 1982; McMaster & Sawkins, 1996; Mueller, 1989). By contrast, if services are contracted out, then the pressures of a competitive market lead to improved performance.

The advocates of service contracting in local government have been influenced strongly by public choice arguments on bureaucracy that were developed in the 1960s(Downs, 1967; Niskanen, 1968, 1971; Tullock, 1965).

For example, Savas(1974: 474) argues that "since most city agencies are monopolies, their staffs are automatically in a position to exercise that monopoly power for their own parochial advantage —and efficiency is rarely seen as an advantage. In short, we have unwittingly built a system in which the public is at the mercy of its servants"(see also Bennett & Johnson, 1979).

The production of public services by external agencies has grown substantially since the early 1970s. As Miranda & Andersen(1994: 28) note, "although the use of contracting varies across service areas, contracts have been used for every service local governments provide." The expansion of contracting out can be viewed as a huge natural experiment that effectively tests the validity of public choice propositions concerning the behavior of public managers who possess monopoly.

This discussion leads to government failure. Government failure, also known as non-market failure, is the public sector version of market failure. The market fails and government intervention causes a more inefficient allocation of goods and resources than would occur without the intervention.

Government failures can occur in relation to both supply and demand within a market. Demand failures are the result of preference/revelation problems and the imbalance of voting and collective behavior.

Supply failures are usually the result of principal-agent problems. In this case, the failure occurs in trying to get one party(agent) to work in the best interest of another party(principal)(Source: Boundless. "Government Failure." Boundless Economics. Boundless, 26 May. 2016. Retrieved 08 Jul. 2016 from https://www.boundless.com/economics/textbooks/boundless-economics-textbook/challenges-to-efficient-outcomes-15/sources-of-inefficiency-83/government-failure-322-12419/).

Figure 9–6 Government Failure

Source: http://latinosreadytovote.com/the-anatomy-of-government-failure/

Markets can also fail. Market failure is an economic term that encompasses a situation where, in any given market, the quantity of a product demanded by consumers does not equate to the quantity supplied by suppliers. This is a direct result of a lack of certain economically ideal factors, which prevents equilibrium.

Market failures have negative effects on the economy because an optimal allocation of resources is not attained. In other words, the social costs of producing the good or service (all of the opportunity costs of the input resources used in its creation) are not minimized, and this results in a waste of some resources.

Take, for example, the common argument against minimum wage laws. Minimum wage laws set wages above the going market-clearing wage in an attempt to raise market wages. Critics argue that this higher wage cost will cause employers to hire fewer minimum-wage employees than before the law was implemented. As a result, more minimum wage workers are left unemployed, creating a social cost and resulting in market failure.

Economists identify the following cases of market failure:

Productive and allocative inefficiency

Markets may fail to produce and allocate scarce resources in the most efficient way.

Monopoly power

Markets may fail to control the abuses of monopoly power.

Information failure

Markets may not provide enough information because, during a market transaction, it may not be in the interests of one party to provide full information to the other party.

Externalities occur when one person's actions affect another person's well-being and the relevant costs and benefits are not reflected in market prices. A positive externality arises when my neighbors benefit from my cleaning up my yard. If I cannot charge them for these benefits, I will not clean the yard as often as they would like(Note that the free-rider problem and positive externalities are two sides of the same coin).

A negative externality arises when one person's actions harm another. When polluting, factory owners may not consider the costs that pollution imposes on others. Markets can fail if there are no property rights and negotiation is costly(The Coase Theorem: Ronald H. Coase, *Biography from the Concise Encyclopedia of Economics*).

Figure 9-7 Example of Negative Externality

Externalities undermine the social benefits of individual selfishness. If selfish consumers do not have to pay producers for benefits, they will not pay; and if selfish producers are not paid, they will not produce. A valuable product fails to appear. The problem is not that one person pays for what someone else gets but that nobody pays and nobody gets, even though the good is worth more than it would cost to produce.

Positive externalities are benefits that are infeasible to charge to provide; negative externalities are costs that are infeasible to charge to not provide. Ordinarily, as Adam Smith explained, selfishness leads markets to produce whatever people want; to get rich, you have to sell what the public is eager to buy.

Research and development is a standard example of a positive externality, air pollution of a negative externality(Public Goods and Externalities, by Tyler Cowen, from the *Concise Encyclopedia of Economics*).

Figure 9-8 Example of Positive Externality

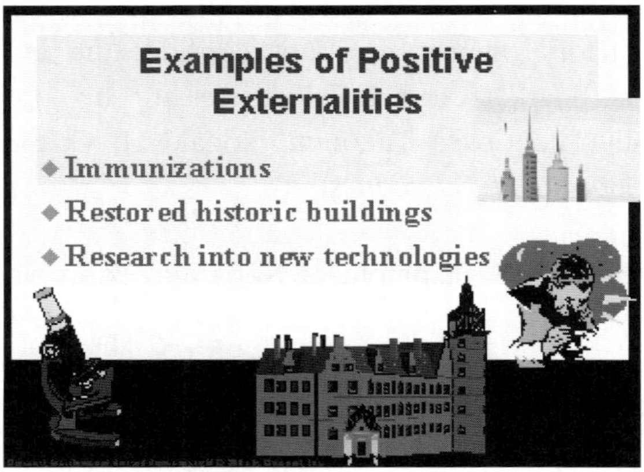

Source: http://www.cameron.edu/~abduls/mpp/chap10/sld007.htm

Most economic arguments for government intervention are based on the idea that the marketplace cannot provide public goods or handle externalities. Public health and welfare programs, education, roads, research and development, national and domestic security, and a clean environment all have been labeled public goods.

Table 9–1 Market Failure and Government Failure

Classification	Market Failure	Government Failure
Reasons	Productive and allocative inefficiency Monopoly Information failure–Principal loss Public Goods–Free–riding Externalities Tragedy of the commons	Log–rolling Bureaucratic pathology Bureaucratic Imperialism Regulation Failure Rent–seeking Captured agency Excessive welfare policy
Remedies	Gov't Regulations	Entrepreneurial Gov't
Results	Regulation Failure, Government Failure	Governance Failure?

Explanation of Major Terms

Public Goods: An item whose consumption is not decided by the individual consumer but by the society as a whole, and which is financed by taxation.

A public good (or service) may be consumed without reducing the amount available for others, and cannot be withheld from those who do not pay for it. Public goods (and services) include economic statistics and other information, law enforcement, national defense, parks, and other things for the use and benefit of all. No market exists for such goods, and they are provided to everyone by governments. Therefore, the problem of free–riding takes place.

Figure 9–9 Examples of Public Goods

	Excludable	Non–excludable
Rival	Private goods Examples: Big Macs Running shoes	Common resources Examples: Tuna in the ocean Public park
Non–rival	Quasl–public goods Examples: Cable TV Toil road	Public goods Examples: National defence Street lighting

Externalities: Factors whose benefits (called external economies) and costs (called external diseconomies) are not reflected in the market price of goods and services.

Externalities are a loss or gain in the welfare of one party resulting from an activity of another party, without there being any compensation for the losing party. Externalities are an important consideration in cost–benefit analysis.

Positive externality is defined as benefits that accrue to a third parties not involved in an economic activity. Negative externalities are costs that third parties has to bear when a good is consumed or produced.

Example of a negative externality that results from consumption is road congestion and pollution. On the other hand, example of a positive externality is that if you walk to work, it will reduce congestion and pollution, benefiting everyone else in the city.

Tragedy of the Commons: a term used to describe what happens to common resources as a result of human greed. It was first coined in an article in Science in 1968 by Garrett Hardin. The commons dilemma was seen long before Hardin, but he brought widespread attention to it and described it in a common–sense fashion that made it easily accessible.

At its core, the Tragedy of the Commons demonstrates that, in an situation where the consequences of a course of action are shared among a collective, while the benefits are reaped by an individual or single group within the collective, people will tend to take actions that in the long term are detrimental to the group as a whole. This is a tragedy because, in seeking their own personal gain, the members of the group actually ultimately hurt themselves.

The example Hardin uses to illustrate the Tragedy of the Commons is of a group of ranchers and a shared land area. Each farmer is assumed to be keeping their own cattle on the land, from which they yield a personal profit, but the land is assumed to be collectively shared, or leased from a government.

Each additional head of cattle has a cost and a gain associated with it: the cost is in land use and wear on the land, while the gain has to do with the profit that can be reaped from that cattle. The trick is, when a rancher adds a cow to his herd, he gains all the benefit of the extra cow, while sharing only a small portion of the cost in terms of land use.

The Tragedy of the Commons can be applied to any sort of common resource, and has been used to describe a number of different situations. Fisheries are one of the most obvious victims, where a single fisherman might be able to fish as much as he or she wished without reaching the limit of a seemingly infinite resource. With tens of thousands of fishermen all pursuing the same strategy, however, the fisheries become depleted and there are no fish for anyone.

Figure 9–10 The Tragedy of the Commons

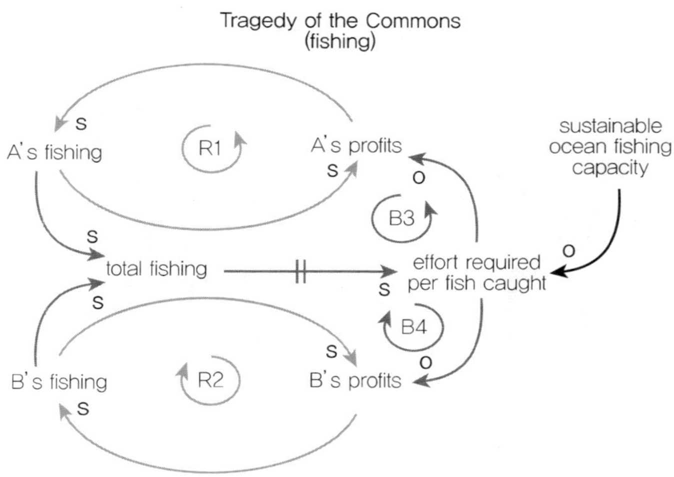

Source: http://roaringdrake.blogspot.kr/2011/09/tragedy-of-commons.html#!/2011/09/tragedy-of-commons.html

Public roads are an excellent example of common property shared by many people. Each of these people has his or her own interest in mind — typically, how to get to work as quickly and easily as possible. But when everyone decides that public roads are the best way to meet traveling needs, the roads jam up and slow down overall traffic movement, filling the air with pollutants from idling cars.

Turning public roads into private roads or toll roads creates a different scenario. With a toll to pay (especially if the toll is higher during peak-use hours such as rush hour), drivers may consider a less-direct route or choose to drive to work at a different time.

Log – rolling: Log – rolling is the trading of favors, or quid pro quo, such as vote trading by legislative members to obtain passage of actions of interest to each legislative member, resulting in the pork – barrel legislation.

Classic examples of such pork – barrel legislation include appropriations bills for highway and airport construction. In organizational analysis, it refers to a practice in which different organizations promote each other's agendas, each in the expectation that the other will reciprocate.

Figure 9–11 Log–rolling

Source: http://what–is–this.net/en/define/logrolling

Rent – seeking: The expenditure of resources in order to bring about an uncompensated transfer of goods or services from another person or persons to one's self as the result of a "favorable" decision on some public policy.

The term seems to have been coined (or at least popularized in contemporary political economy) by the economist Gordon Tullock. Examples of rent – seeking behavior would include all of the various ways by which individuals or groups lobby government for taxing, spending and regulatory policies that confer financial benefits or other special advantages upon them at the expense of the taxpayers or of consumers or of other groups or individuals with which the beneficiaries may be in economic competition.

Captured Agency: A government agency, especially a regulatory agency, that is largely under the influence of the economic interest groups. A captured agency shapes its regulations and policies primarily to benefit these favored client groups rather than public interest at the expense of less organized and often less influential groups such as consumers.

Table 9-2 Comparison of Paradigms in Summary

Paradigm	Politics/Adm. Indivisibility	Politics/ Adm. Dichotomy	Principles of PA	New Dichotomy	PA as Mgt.	PA as PA	Fm Gov't to Governance
Period	Early 19c.	1880s~ 1910s	1910s~ 1930s	1940s~ 1960s	1950s~ 1970s	1970s~ 1990s	1990s~
Theory Approach	Legal	Classical OT	Neo-classical OT	Behavioral, Systems Theory	NPA	NPM	Governance
Personnel Adm	Spoils System	Merit System	Merit System	Merit System	Merit Affirmative Action	Merit System	Merit System
Adm. Values	Legality	Efficiency	Higher-level of Efficiency	Efficiency	Social Equity	Productivity	Respon-siveness, Responsi-bility
Scholars	Wilson Goodnow	Weber Taylor Gulick	Mayo Maslow	Simon Sharkansky Riggs	Frederickson	Osborne Gaebler	Peters

TOEIC for Chapter 9.

01 Systems theory can be _____ all types of systems at all levels in all fields of research.

(A) applied for (B) applied to
(C) applied on (D) applied

Key Point

1. 자동사/타동사의 활용이 틀린 문제가 아주 많다.

타동사인 데 뒤에 전치사를 쓴 문제와 자동사인 데도 불구하고 뒤에 전치사를 쓰지 않은 문제들이 자주 출제가 된다.

- 다음과 같은 완전 타동사는 ( )안에 있는 전치사를 쓰지 않도록 주의한다. reach ~~(to)~~, contact ~~(with)~~, call ~~(to)~~, treat ~~(with)~~, discuss ~~(about)~~, marry ~~(with)~~, attend ~~(to)~~, join ~~(into)~~, enter ~~(to)~~, exceed ~~(at)~~ 초과하다, 능가하다, await ~~(for)~~ 기다리다
- 반대로, 아래의 동사들은 자동사로, 꼭 뒤의 전치사와 함께 쓰여야 한다. deal with, talk about, care for ~를 돌보다, interfere with ~에 간섭하다, 개입하다

해설 apply to 적용하다, apply for 지원하다
따라서 답은 (B) applied to

02 They get access to _____ .

(A) many informations (B) much information
(C) few information (D) many information

해설 수량형용사 Many, Much
many, few 다음에는 복수명사
much, little 다음에는 단수명사
◇ I have many things to do today.
She has much information.
◇ He has had to spend a good deal of money on medicines.
◇ She spends a lot of money on clothes.
information은 불가산 명사이므로 단수이다.
따라서 2번 답은 (B) much information

Vocabulary for TOEIC

1. input = enter = flow into
2. conversion = transform = change
3. output = produce = flow out
4. feedback = flow backward
5. entropy = the degree of disorder or uncertainty in a system
6. negentropy = reverse entropy. which means things become more in order
7. homeostasis = the property of a system, which keeps it balanced, stable, or not subject to change
8. equifinality = the property of allowing or having the same effect or result from different events
9. diffract = refract = bend = curve
10. systems theory
11. fused = blended = converged
12. prismatic
13. advocate = support
14. agricultural
15. tenet = doctrine
16. parochial = partisan
17. government failure
18. market failure
19. externality
20. log－rolling = supporting a bill
21. tragedy of the commons
22. greed = lust = desire
23. illustrate = explain by examples
24. rent = lease a house

References

Kaufmann, Daniel, Aart Kraay, & Pablo Zoido－Lobaton(2002). “Governance Matters Ⅱ: Updated Indicators for 2000－01.” *Policy Research Working Paprer 2772.* Washington: World Bank.

OECD(1996). *Integrating People management into Public Service Reform.* Raris: Publication Service.

Osborne, David & Ted Gaebler(1992). *Reinventing Government: How the Entrepreneurial Spirit in Transforming the Public Sector.* New York: Addison－Wesley Pub.

Ostrom, Vincent(1974). *The Intellectual Crisis in American Public Administration*, Revised edition. Alabama: University of Alabama Press.

Peters, B. G.(1998). *The Future of Governing: Four Emerging Models.* Lawrence, Kansas: University Press of Kansas.

Riggs, Fred W.(1957). Agraria and Industria. Toward a Typology of Comparative Administration. In: Siffin William J. (ed.) *Toward the Comparative Study of Public Administration.* Indiana, USA: Bloomington.

______(1961). *The Ecology of Public Administration*. New Delhi. Bombay: Asia Publishing House.

Part 1. Fundamentals of Public Administration Cases

1. How can you define public administration?
2. Discuss the study of public administration made by Woodrow Wilson.
3. Explain the evolution of public administration paradigms.
4. Explain the approaches to public administration.
5. Explain the systems theory.
6. Explain the public goods.
7. Explain the Tragedy of the Commons.
8. Explain the log-rolling.
9. Explain the positive externality and negative externality.
10. Explain the ecological system approach.

Class Exercise

The Reinventing Government

Team A: Bureaucrats and Citizens(Con: Keep status quo)
Team B: Bureaucrats and Big Business(Pro: Make change)

Issue: Privatization of the Department of Public Services of the city of White Bluff, Oregon. Organizational chart for areas of service attached.

Moderators: 2

Moderators: Toss coin to see which team begins. Each team presents for 5~8 minutes. Another 5 minutes for rebuttals of additional arguments. Keep order. Keep proceedings civil.

Teams: Choose a recorder to keep notes of your meeting and a spokesperson to present the arguments. Everyone else on the team, be alert to assist the spokesperson as needed. Use the board as needed.

1. Argue for Pro and Con

Politics–Administration Dichotomy — Can politics and administration really remain separate in public bureaucracies?(Pro and Con)

Power Issues in the Bureaucracy — Special interest power versus public interest power issues(Pro and Con)

Ethics Issues — Is it ever acceptable for public administrators to "dirty their hands" for the public good?(Pro and Con)

Arguments: Speak to the benefits of your position; costs of the opposing position.

Part 2 Organizations

What I have noticed about bureaucratic programs is that for all their rules and red tape, they keep very little track of what actually happens to the people they are serving.

—Tom Fulton

In Part 2, we lay basic foundations on the issues related to public organizations. In Chapter 1, we look at the necessity of organizations. In Chapter 2, the various definitions of organizations including not only traditional definitions but metaphorical ones are searched for.

And in Chapter 3, we try to track the changes of organization theories and to find out how they have been changed in various ways, ranging from classical organization theory and neo-classical organization theory to structural contingency theory. Finally chaos and self-organization is touched on.

01 Chapter Why Do We Need Organizations?

Bureaucracies are designed to perform public business. But as soon as a bureaucracy is established, it develops an autonomous spiritual life and comes to regard the public as its enemy.

— Brooks Atkinson

LEARNING OBJECTIVES

After reading Chapter 1, the student should be able to:

1. Understand the necessity of organization.
2. Understand the types of communication networks.
3. Understand the characteristics of communication networks.

Organizations play an important role in modern societies. They function as critical means to achieve individual goals in social, political, economic and many other areas. Private organizations produce, process, and sell various consumption goods and services to make our lives more comfortable. Public organizations protect us from crimes, insecure consumptive goods and contaminated air and water. And they provide us with national defense against foreign invasion, construction and maintenance of roads and airports, education of our offspring and various services to improve our general quality of life.

However there are also many dark sides in the organizations in the modern society. That's because most of the bad things for humans are made through modern organizations. Illegal and dangerous drugs, suppression of human rights all around the world, and the toxic chemical wastes are another organizational byproducts. For the individuals, they must the burden to comply and obey to the goals of the organizations to which they belong sacrificing their own goals.

From the times of Karl Marx until now many authors have insisted that dehumanization and specialization which characterize modern organizations caused workers stress and ultimately alienation. In case of political system, the necessity to depend on large scale bureaucratic organization to perform public policies raised problems of responsiveness and responsibility of information in all levels.

No matter how the total contribution of organizations to modern society might be evaluated, understanding of organizations and of how they operate will be one of the most significant factors in determining the survival, success and happiness of both individual and society. The roles of organizations are equally important not only to public administration but also to public policy. Public administration is the management of organizations and people in organizations, and almost all the public policies are implemented by organizations. Therefore it's necessary to understand public organizations and to improve them in order to maintain and upgrade the quality of delivery system of public services as an alternative to ever deepening financial scarcity in modern public administration.

1. The Necessity of Organizations: From the View-point of Social Network Theory

It's generally said that the whole is greater than the sum of its parts. Constituent parts are interconnected into structure; that is to say, social networks. This functional structure has more number of relations than before they are structured. This explanation is similar to that of structural functionalism. While the number of organizational members increase arithmetically, the number of relations among organizational members increase geometrically.

$$r = nC_2 = \frac{n(n-1)}{2}$$

n =number of organizational members
r =number of relations among organizational members

But the number of relations among organizational members is not the number of real relationships, but just the number of potential relationships. The number of real relationships can increase much more depending on organizational management.

In case of chain and wheel types of communication network which can be said to be a centralized network that is effective for simple problems, all the information is passed through a central position in a top-down manners. On the other hand, in case of circle and all-channel forms of communication network which can be said to be a decentralized network that is effective for complex problems, all the information flow not only vertically but also horizontally.

Figure 1-1 Types of Communication Network

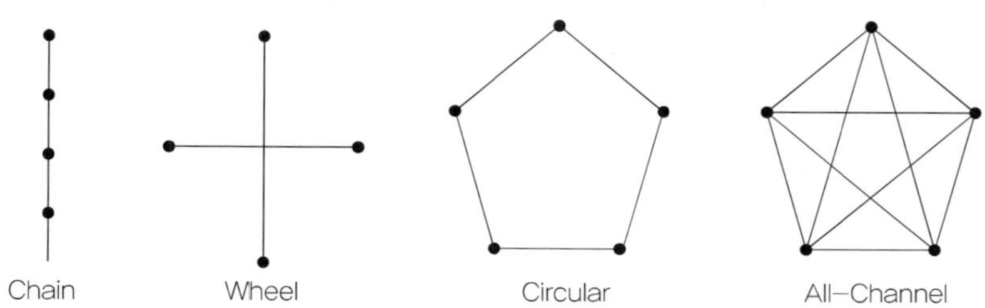

The more a communication network is centralized, the faster the speed of problem solving is in simple problems, but the slower in complex problems. And vice versa. And the more a communication network is centralized, the more accurate the accuracy of problems solving is, but the less accurate in complex problems.

Finally the more a communication network is centralized, the lower the members of the group satisfaction is. On the contrary, the more a communication network is decentralized, the higher the members of the group satisfaction is.

Figure 1–2 The Characteristics of Group Communication Networks

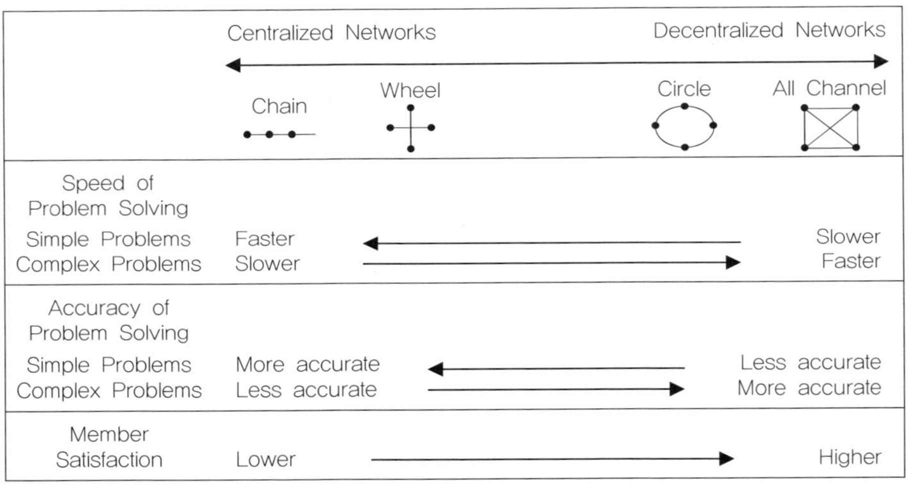

Source: Alex Bavelas, & Dermot Barrett(1951). *An Experimental Approach to Organizational Communication*, New York, American Management Association.

Since organizational charts which can only represent formal structure of organization are unable to fully reflect the networks inside the organization, they only show outer parts of complex organizational reality. Despite the fact that the structure and networks of organization inseparable, studies on organizations have primarily focused on the formal structure of organizations.

Let's look into the organization management principles of administrative management school that is classified as one of classical organization theories. The reasons why the unity of command principle that subordinates should get orders only from one superior and top–down or downward communication are intendedly emphasized to control the pattern and the direction of organizational networks. So the centralized networks such as the wheel form go well with efficiency-oriented classical organization theory.

Human relations theory begins to regard informal groups and bottom-up communication as important, which implies attention to informal connections and interconnections in organizational networks. However both classical and neo-classical organizational theorists failed to grasp organizations as networks.

Simon, a behaviouralist, insists on the descriptive analysis of the decision-making process rather than the provision of the prescriptive management principles, pinpointing the contradictions among classical management principles just as if many proverbs are contradicting. For instance, the principle of span of control might decrease the horizontal relational complexity, but increases vertical hierarchy of command, ultimately generating much bigger problem of coordination.

Weber who predicted bureaucracy insisted that the more exclusion of individual, emotional, and irrational elements from bureaucracy, the more perfect bureaucracy. This means that relational strength among features of networks are gotten rid of. But the scholars who put emphasis on cultural effects think such characteristics as density, clustering, interconnectedness (political-industrial interconnectedness, or plutocracy), and strength (such personal ties as kinship, sectionalism, alumni relationships) of networks as important factors.

02 Chapter

The Definitions and Types of Organization

Management is doing things right; leadership is doing the right things

—Peter F. Drucker

LEARNING OBJECTIVES

After reading Chapter 2, the student should be able to:

1. Understand the traditional definition of organizations.
2. Understand the various images or metaphors of organizations.

1. Traditional Definition of Organizations

Classical organization theory posits that organizational goals can be divided into specific tasks (specification and specialization based on the division of labour) by means of rational methods, and they can also be reassembled (integration and coordination) to accomplish organization–wide goals. It can be said that this line of concept springs from Newtonian mechanical paradigm, which holds simplistic and orderly world view based on the principle of atomism and mechanism that the whole can be divided into atom and the atom can be reassembled into the whole. This thought is the fundamental system of thought which influenced the modern society at large. From the view–point of organization theory, Weber firmly believed that legal–rational bureaucracy based on this paradigm will be dominant, which is historically inevitable.

It's commonly said that an organization is a cooperative system of social units equipped with an activity system of division of labour and integration to achieve a certain common goal rationally. It's conceptual features are goal–orientation, rational activity system of division of labour and integration, social units including structure and process, and interaction with environments with a certain boundary.

Judging from the previous definition of organization, administrative organization can be defined as social units with an activity system of division of labour and integration to achieve a certain common administrative goal. The category of an administrative organization covers national administrative organizations, local governments, public enterprises, the National Assembly, the Court, and the Constitutional Court.

2. A New Interpretation of Organizations

Imaginization is more important than knowledge.
Creative imaginization is necessary to pose a new question and possibility, and to view existing problem from a new angle.

– Albert Einstein –

Figure 2–1 Organization is Imagination

포드(Henry Ford)는 도축장에서 돼지, 소들이 걸려 있는 이동식 벨트를 보고 자동차 컨베이어벨트 아이디어를 떠올렸다.

Since in many situations organizational goal is hard to agree on, and it can be said to be a conflicting goal rather than a common goal. And it also might be said to be a conflict system rather than cooperative system. Therefore, we can say that an organization is a conflict system consisting of more than 2 people to rationally or sometimes irrationally achieve conflicting goals. This definition might describe the realities of organizational life. We try to introduce more definitions of organizations.

Morgan's book is based on the premise that almost all our thinking about organizations is based on one or more of eight basic metaphors.

1) Organization as a Machine based on the Newtonian Mechanical Paradigm

This is the most simplistic metaphor, and is the foundation of Taylorism and Fordism. An organization like a machine metaphor is mostly used by managers when they want to express the idea of their units "running smoothly as a well–oiled machine." Morgan for instance, deems Frederick the Great of Prussia the one who, in practice, firstly used this model in that he organised his army as a model of mechanistic organization.

Organization as a machine metaphor is well described and symbolized in the famous movie Modern Times by Chaplin where an organizational member is regarded as cog in a machine, resulting in the dehumanization and impersonality.

Figure 2–2 Organization as a Machine

2) Organization as an Evolving Organism

Organization as Organism: This is a slightly richer metaphor and suggests such ideas as "organizational DNA," birth, maturity and death, and so forth. An organization is a living system which is living in a wider environments pursuing satisfaction of various needs.

A organization from this perspective has an image of organism interacting continually with the environments, and enables us to have open and flexible views on an organization.

Amoeba–like organizations are geared to foster ability, personality, and potential of organizational members based upon the belief that large organization is operated as collectives of small business units. Organization is far from a concrete, reorganization and spin–offs are occurring frequently with the help of autonomy and flexibility.

Maintaining the principle that any organization only have one function and goal, new spin–offs are made if new functions or goals are added. They consists of 2 to several hundreds, but usually is composed of 10 people. All the authority including finance is empowered to them.

Figure 2–3 Organization as an Evolving Organism

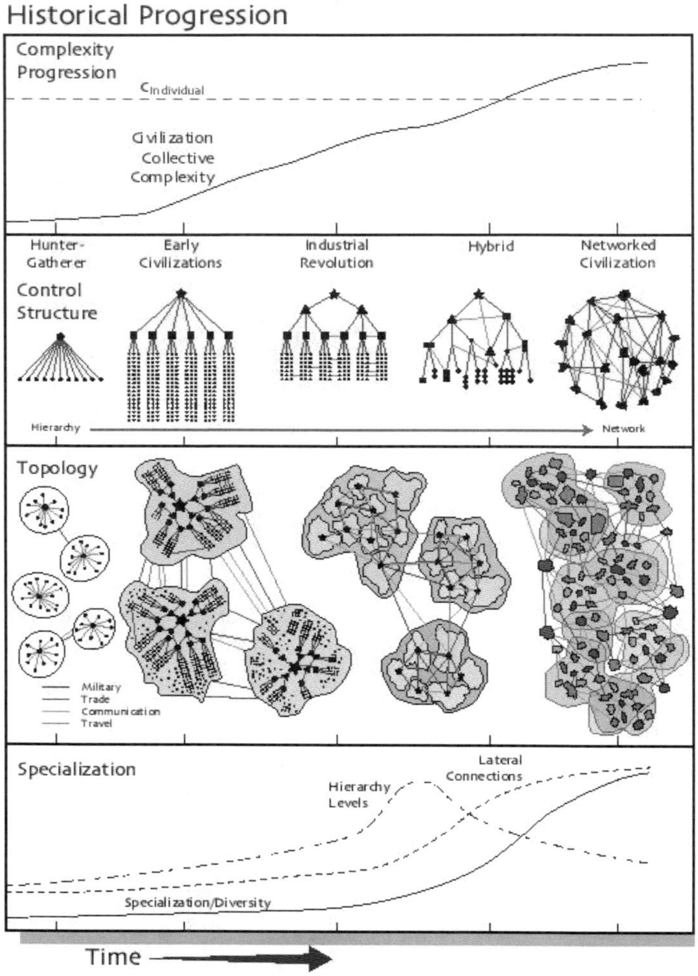

3) Organization as a Information–processing Brain

Organization as Brain: This may sound like a subset of the Organism metaphor (and there is some overlap), but there is a subtle and important shift in emphasis from "life processes" to learning.

You must have heard slim organization. In information society organizations are moving from slim–form toward network–form organizations which got rid of trunk, arms and legs, remaining only brain. For instance Amazon distributes books using FedEx or DHL, and abolished even bookstores.

We tend to think of organizations as a firm concrete. So once they are solidated, they become as stiff as a stone, even though they were as flexible as fluid. Is it impossible to have dynamically flexible organizations that self-organize with flexibility like a fluid metal?

Self-organizing virtual organization does not have a concrete form unlike fluid. It's vitality is in the flexibility that can adjust its form rapidly according to the demands of customers.

Figure 2-4 Organization as an Information-processing Brain

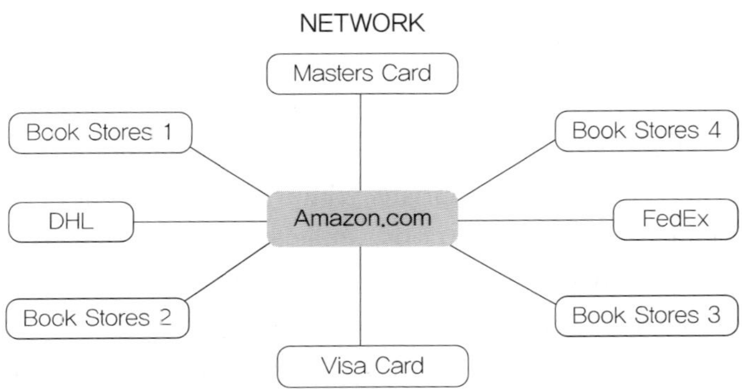

4) Organization as a Psychic Prison

Morgan uses the proper symbol to explain an organization as a psychic prison. It is the Plato's cave symbol, claiming that knowledge gained through the 5 senses is no more than opinion and that, in order to have real knowledge, we must gain it through philosophical reasoning.

Max Weber, a founder of machine bureaucracy, predicting the dominance of the rational-legal bureaucracy in society, warned the possibility of bureaucracy falling into the iron cage due to bureaucratic dysfunctions. It can mold the bureaucratic members way of thought like a prison without cage.

Figure 2–5 Organization as a Psychic Prison

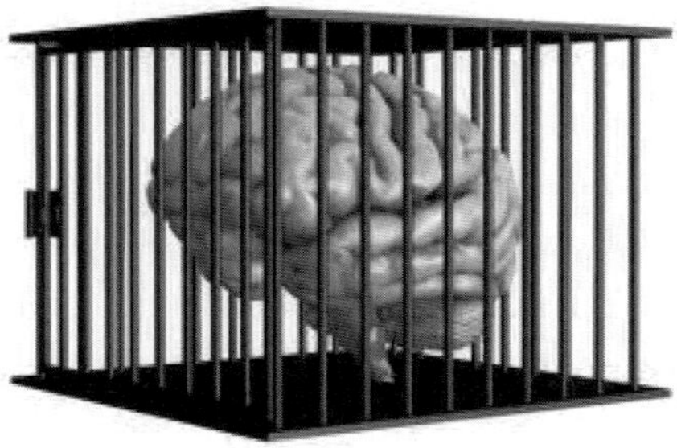

5) Organization as a Culture

Organization as a Culture may help explaining what the most important objective of corporate culture is. Organizational culture is a system of shared assumptions, values, and beliefs that helps individuals understand which behaviors are and are not appropriate within an organization.

It also includes an shared actions, beliefs, custom, way of doing things expectations, experiences, feelings, …… philosophy, rituals, symbols, way of thinking, understanding, and values and so forth. How would you define organization culture? Describe its various features and manifestations. Sometimes culture functions as a cage which captures and shapes all the features of culture; that is, our action, belief, custom, ideology, knowledge, norms, and thoughts, etc.

6) Organization as a Means to Domination and Exploitation

The death of a salesman by Arthur Miller is a story about a wife who worships the deceased husband and 60–year–old salesman Willie with two sons idling away. He relies on the dreams and hopes of youth, and he is an ordinary man leading a hard company life with the heavy burden of breeding a family.

Conflicts among family members, a heavy burden of feeding family in a brutality of a society finally force him into death. And this story suggests the problems we are facing now or will be living in the contemporary age. The success in the capitalistic society means the accumulation of wealth. The survival of the fittest or the law of jungle that one can only survive when he outwins the severe competitive race applies. So the theme of this play is to beat the competitor regardless of means and methods.

This story illustrates how organizations exploit and utilize the members of the organizations. When members are needed, they are utilized, and when they are not wanted they are deserted. And this also explains how OT emphasizes close relationships among organizations, class and control.

Usually we draw organization structure as a pyramid, imagine the construction of pyramids in Egypt. Just imagine how many people were managed, controled, and exploited to build pyramids.

Figure 2–6 Pyramids of Egypt

Figure 2–7 Metaphors of Organization

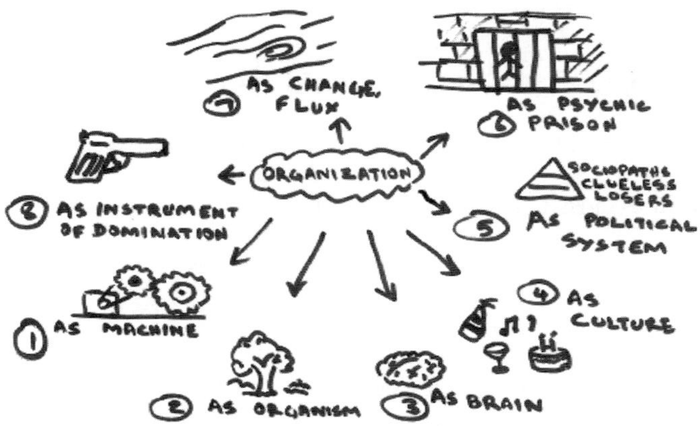

Source: Morgan, Gareth(1997). *Images of Organisation*. Sage.

03
Chapter

The Changes of Organization Theory Paradigms

Crazy times call for crazy organizations.

—Tom Peters

LEARNING OBJECTIVES

After reading Chapter 3, the student should be able to:

1. Understand the evolutionary nature of organization theories.
2. Understand the classical organization theories.
3. Understand the neo-classical organization theories.
4. Understand the motivation theories.
5. Understand the leadership theories.
6. Understand the structural contingency theories.

Organization theory(OT) as a general field of study has a relatively short history. That's because attention to the necessity of organization theory has been paid only after organizations came to play an important role in society. As organizations develop and the sphere is widening, organization theory emerges as academic and practical field of research that reflects basic interests in organization management, attempting to determine bests methods to structure and run organizations.

The fundamental value pursued by OT is to maximize organizational rationality, which is narrowly defined as the ratio of outputs to inputs, or efficiency (Some theorists are still defining it narrowly). Early approach to OT focuses on the structural aspects in that structure completely controls the behaviour of individual workers, and the development of use of perfect structure will get rid of the necessity of attention to individuals.

The shifts in OT perspectives can be divided into 1) classical OT and neo-classical OT based on closed system theory, 2) adaptation view, enactment view, natural selection view, interaction view between organization and environment based upon open system theory and contingency theory, 3) self-organization view based on chaos theory.

Figure 3-1 Evolution of Organization Management Thought

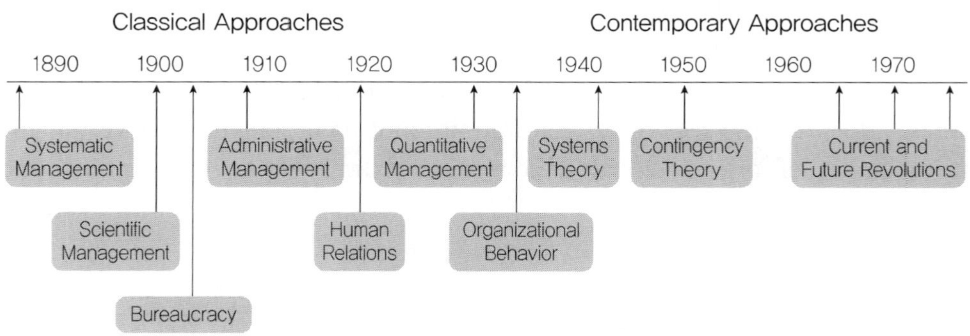

One of the concepts shaping systemic view is that of open and closed system. Closed system is a metaphor depicting self-contained entity whose objective is to study the functions of the constituent parts and their interactions. Here relationship with the environment is regulated and stabilized by analytically neglecting environment in describing and controling a system.

This is similar to what Weber has done in describing the characteristics of ideal type bureaucracy.

This view is based on the assumption that environmental support is predictable rather than problematic. So the resources for the system is utilized for the maintenance of the equilibrium and homeostasis, and the focus is on the internal efficiency.

Modern theorists do not speak for closed system approach any more. This is just a labelling for the theoretical view that pays no attention to relation between system and external environment.

From the perspective of systems theory which is equilibrium model, organizations are thought of as self-regulating system maintaining system equilibrium through feedback that is the function of correcting deviations from a standard and norm. Positive feedback, or deviation-amplifying feedback triggers changes in a system, while negative feedback, or deviation-counteracting feedback maintains homeostasis along with pattern maintenance function, latency function; that is, built-in stabilizer.

A system is a set of constituent parts interconnected functionally, and should be understood in a holistic view. And since it's a self-regulating system maintaining system equilibrium through feedback, stability and inertia due to negative feedback and built-in stabilizers is dominant.

Even though conflicts exist, they can be institutionalized or ultimately eliminated. Organization changes take place gradually from external environments. Most of theories on organization and environment believe in the improvement of organizational effectiveness if fit between organization and environment is maintained.

1. Closed System Theory: Classical Organization Theory and Neo-classical Organization Theory

<Table 3-1> shows the typology of OT categorized based on the locus of organizational change. It's categorized based on the two dimensions, 1) whether theory is prescriptive or descriptive, 2) the relationship between system and environment.

Classical OT in Quadrant I posits that organizational goal can be divided into specific tasks, and at the same time these tasks can be reassembled into organization−wide goal.

Table 3-1 Typology of Organization Theory

System / Theory	Closed Artificial System	Open Natural System	Self-Organizing System
	Ⅰ. Structure	Ⅲ. Human Relations	Ⅴ. Self-Organization
Descriptive	· Vertical Command · Hierarchy of authority · Specialization, Routinization based on Division of labour · Economic Incentive · Direction · Classical OT	· Moral · Informal Group · Routine works cause stress · Noneconomic Incentive · Motivation · Human Relations	· Redundancy · Requisite Variety · Minimum Specification · Learning to learn · Self-Organizing · Holography
	Ⅱ. Operations Analysis	Ⅳ. Interaction Analysis	Ⅵ. Self-Organizing Process
Prescriptive	· Specification of Problems · Comparison of Alternatives based on C/B Analysis · Routinization · Decision-making Theory	· Interactive Effects between Organizations and Environments · Contradictary Conflicts are natural · Organizational Goal is Adaptation · Lamarckian Adaptation Darwinian Selection Dialectical Analysis	· Environmental Change within Bifurcation Point · Environmental Change outside Bifurcation Point · Order out of Chaos · Self-Organization Dissipative Structure

These earlier approaches began to be known as classical OT. Well−known theorists or administrators in classical OT are Frederick W. Taylor, M. Weber, Lyndall F. Urwick, Luther Gulick, James Mooney, Alan Reilly, and Henri Fayol, and so forth. They held a common belief that organization management is a science, universally applicable laws or principles can be determined, and most efficient organizations can be made by these.

Taylor, in his book entitled The Principles of Scientific Management, emphasized an analysis of task process primarily by means of time and motion study to determine "one best way" to perform all tasks in an organization. Once one best way is determined, the next step of the managers is to select and train workers scientifically to complete tasks with one best way.

Four principles of Scientific Management are;

1. develop a scientific approach for each element of one's work
2. scientifically select, train, teach and develop each worker
3. cooperate with workers to ensure that jobs match plans and principles
4. ensure appropriate division of labor

Taylor has been criticized for looking down on the complications and intricacies of the workers' motivation. Taylor argues that workers and managers can and must share common interests. Common interests are high wages for workers and high profits for the managers, so the focus is on the money. Nevertheless Taylor's approach to workers is basically not humanistic.

Other classical OT focuses on the principles of organization structure. The concepts are mainly span of control, unity of command, scalar chain, division of labour, and organizing by purpose, process, place and customers. Just as Taylor had a firm belief that there must be one best way to perform a task, they also firmly believed that there must be one best way to design organization structure. Consequently they had been criticized for too simple and unrealistic approach.

Figure 3-2 Command and Control & Top-down

One of the most severe criticism originated from that of Herbert Simon insisting convincingly that the scientific principles were like proverbs. We can find contradicting principles for most principles. In spite of these criticisms these principles have been playing important roles in modern OT.

An argument for the strong Executive whose power is strengthened by hierarchical command and restrictive span of control still remains as an important issue of reforming the State and the Federal government. That's because democratic responsibility can be improved by centralizing responsibility to a few bureaus.

The organizational structure which stems from sticking to the principles of administrative management is classical bureaucracy that is defined and described in the works of Max Weber. An analysis of the ideal type bureaucracy of Weber laid foundation for the later OT. Weber's papers on the bureaucracy published in 1921 are translated into English only after the late 1920'.

As bureaucracy is spreading widely, organization theorists realize that dysfunctions of bureaucracy come from it's very merits. Rules, Impersonality, fixed system of command, and specialization which are characterisitcs of bureaucracy give birth to red-tape, dehumanization, rigidity, and tedious and unsatisfactory jobs. When a bureaucracy falls into this situation, the rationality and efficiency of the bureaucracy decreases, and the mission of the OT becomes to find out the solutions to dysfunctions inherent in the bureaucracy.

> Gettysburg address is made up of 226 words.
> The Ten Commandments are composed of 297 words.
> The regulations of the U.S Dept. of Agriculture on the cabbage price is 15629 words.

> People seldom try to think when there are 100 people.
> They try to think when there are only 4 to 8 people.
> —Annonymous CEO—

With the increase in the dehumanization tendency of classical OT, organizational humanism focusing on the human side of enterprise begins to emerge. Even if a series of humanistic movement tried to enhance humanistic factors, it itself failed to reach a humanistic goal and just remained as humanistic means to achieve organizational goal.

One of the first attempts to discover the answer was human relations approach by Elton Mayo, Fritz Roethlisberger, & William Dickson. The core organizational concept to Weber and classical OT is machine bureaucracy, and humans working in that machine tend to be regarded as important but as exchangeable parts of the machine.

Human relations theorists consider organizations as social system consisting of attitudes, values, beliefs and behaviours of the individual shaped by groups in side an organization or informal groups as well as factors outside of an organization.

As the focus of the OT is moving toward informal organizations, formal organizations also attempt to understand and make use of these informal organizations for the purpose of achieving goals.

Common features of both classical OT based on Newtonian mechanical paradigm and neo-classical OT (Human Relations Theory) are that good principles of administrative management are universally applicable to all types of organizations, based on the assumption that all organizations are alike.

Decision-making school such as Simon, pointing out the fact that management principles might be contradictory like proverbs, insist that the focus of the organizational analysis should be changed from the suggestion of prescriptive management principles to the analysis of descriptive decision-making process.

In reaction to the structure side of the organization, Douglas McGregor described Theory X and Theory Y in his book, The Human Side of Enterprise.

Theory X and Theory Y

Theory X and Theory Y each represent different ways in which leaders view employees. Theory X managers believe that employees are motivated mainly by money, are lazy, uncooperative, and have poor work habits. Theory Y managers believe that subordinates work hard, are cooperative, and have positive attitudes.

Theory X is the traditional view of direction and control by managers.

1. The average human being has an inherent dislike of work and will avoid if he or she can.

2. Because of this human characteristic of dislike of work, most people must be controlled, directed, and threatened with punishment to get them to put forth adequate effort toward the achievement of organizational objectives.
3. The average human being prefers to be directed, wishes to avoid responsibility, has relatively little ambition, wants security above all.

Theory X leads naturally to an emphasis on the tactics of control for telling people what to do and for administering rewards and punishment. Theory X explains the consequences of a particular managerial strategy. Because its assumptions are so unnecessarily limiting, it prevents managers from seeing the possibilities inherent in other managerial strategies. As long as the assumptions of Theory X influence managerial strategy, organizations will fail to discover, let alone utilize, the potentialities of the average human being.

Theory Y is the view that individual and organizational goals can be integrated.

1. The expenditures of physical and mental effort in work are as natural as play or rest.
2. External control and the threat of punishment are not the only means for bringing out effort toward organizational objectives.
3. Commitment to objectives is a function of the rewards associated with their achievement.
4. The average human being learns, under proper conditions, not only to accept but also to seek responsibility.
5. The capacity to exercise a relatively high degree of imagination, ingenuity, and creativity in the solution of organizational problems in widely, not narrowly, distributed in the population.
6. Under the condition of modern industrial life, the intellectual potentialities of the average human being are only partially utilized.

Theory Y's purpose is to encourage integration, to create a situation in which an employee can achieve his or her own goals best by directing his or her efforts toward the objectives of the organization.

Human relations school produced various theories on motivation and leadership. Why and what exactly employees want and need, why they behave and what satisfies them were all still something mysterious. It's like a black box and it hasn't been fully revealed. Overall, the basic perspective on motivation looks something like this:

Figure 3–3 Basic Perspective on Motivation

In other words, you have certain needs or wants (these terms will be used interchangeably), and this causes you to do certain things (behavior), which satisfy those needs (satisfaction).

1) Motivation

Neo-classical OT including human relations theory which emerged as an alternative to classical OT that has been criticized as organization without people produced a variety of motivation theories, shifting from direction, command and control-oriented bureaucratic organization to motivating organizational members. For example, there are need hierarchy theory of Maslow, manifested need theory of Murray, ERG theory of Alderfer, XY Theory of McGregor, Two-Factor Theory of Hertzberg, and management system theory of Likert.

(1) Need Hierarchy Theory of Maslow

Goal-directed actions of human is activated by the strongest needs and the consequent motivation among human needs. Scholars who have studied on the human actions in organizations recognized this fact, and they tried to find out the most significant needs common to human being to systematically apply those needs to real organizations.

Abraham Maslow(1954) attempted to synthesize a large body of research related to human motivation. Prior to Maslow, researchers generally focused separately on such factors as biology, achievement, or power to explain what energizes, directs, and sustains human behavior. Maslow posited a hierarchy of human needs based on two groupings: deficiency needs and growth needs.

Within the deficiency needs, each lower need must be met before moving to the next higher level. Once each of these needs has been satisfied, if at some future time a deficiency is detected, the individual will act to remove the deficiency. The first four levels are:

1) Physiological: hunger, thirst, bodily comforts, etc.;
2) Safety/security: out of danger;
3) Belongingness and Love: affiliate with others, be accepted; and
4) Esteem: to achieve, be competent, gain approval and recognition.
5) Self−actualization: to find self−fulfillment and realize one's potential, to have a concern about personal growth and to incorporate an ongoing freshness of appreciation of life.

Table 3−2 Needs of Maslow Explained Easy

Need	Home	Job
Self−actualization	education, religion, hobbies, personal growth	training, advancement, growth, creativity
Esteem	approval of family, friends, community	recognition, high status, responsibilities
Belongingness	family, friends, clubs	teams, depts, coworkers, clients, supervisors, subordinates
Safety	freedom from war, poison, violence	work safety, job security, health insurance
Physiological	food water sex	heat, air, base salary

According to Maslow, an individual is ready to act upon the growth needs if and only if the deficiency needs are met.

Maslow published his first conceptualization of his theory over 50 years ago(Maslow, 1943) and it has since become one of the most popular and often cited theories of human motivation. An interesting phenomenon related to Maslow's work is that in spite of a lack of evidence to support his hierarchy, it enjoys wide acceptance.

(2) The Integration of Motivation Theories

Alderfer(1972) categorized Maslow's 5 needs into 3 needs such as ERG (Existence, Relatedness, and Growth) which was called ERG theory. His approach modified Maslow's theory based on the work of Gordon Allport

(1960, 1961) who incorporated concepts from systems theory into his work on personality.

Herzberg recategorized Maslow's 5 needs into 2 factors such as hygience and motivation which is called two-factor theory. According to Herzberg, there are some job factors that result in satisfaction while there are other job factors that prevent dissatisfaction.

Job factors that result in satisfaction are motivating factors, which include esteem and self-actualization needs. While job factors that prevent dis-satisfaction are hygiene factors, which include physiological, safety and social needs as mentioned above.

Figure 3-4 Integration of Motivation Theories

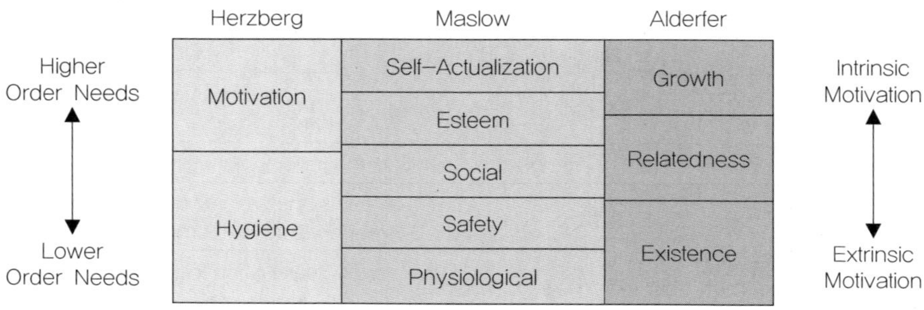

(3) The Process Theories of Motivation

Whereas the content theories concentrate on the question of 'what' motivates, the process theories address more the issues relating to how the process works and sustains itself over time.

Adams equity motivation theory suggested that an employee compares his ratio of output to input to that of referent other.

Figure 3-5 Adams Equity Theory

Person **Referent Other**

$$\frac{\text{Outcomes}}{\text{Inputs}} = \frac{\text{Outcomes}}{\text{Inputs}}$$

Equity theory is based in the idea that individuals are motivated by fairness, and if they identify inequities in the inputs such as efforts and specs or outputs such as wages and promotion ratios of themselves and their referent groups, they will seek to adjust their inputs or outputs to reach their perceived equity.

The expectancy theory of Vroom(1964) defines motivation as a process governing choices among alternative forms of voluntary activities, a process controlled by the individual. The individual makes choices based on estimates of how well the expected results of a given behavior are going to match up with or eventually lead to the desired results. Motivation is a product of the individual's expectancy that a certain effort will lead to the intended performance, the instrumentality of this performance to achieving a certain outcome, and the importance or desirability of this outcome for the individual, known as valence.

In sum, it can expressed a formula as followings;

$$\begin{aligned}\text{Motivational Force(MF)} &= \text{Expectancy} \times \text{Instrumentality} \times \text{Valence} \\ &= (E \rightarrow P) \times (P \rightarrow O) \times \text{Importance of Outcome} \\ &= (\text{Effort} \rightarrow \text{Performance}) \times (\text{Performance} \rightarrow \\ &\quad \text{Outcome}) \times \text{Importance of Outcome}\end{aligned}$$

2) Leadership

Leadership theories can be traced back from trait theory to behavioral theories such as Ohio State Univ., Univ. of Michigan and Managerial Grid to Contingency Theory, and finally to contemporary theories.

Trait Theory(1930's~1940's)

The trait leadership theory believes that people are either born or are made with certain qualities that will make them excel in leadership roles. That is, certain qualities such as charisma, intelligence, sense of responsibility, creativity and other values puts anyone in the shoes of a good leader such as Hitler and Napoleon.

However trait theory is criticized for the lack of valid empirical studies. Resultantly, the behavioral theories emerged.

Behavioral Theories

The behavioral theorists identified determinants of leadership so that people could be trained to be leaders. They developed training programs to change managers' leadership behaviors and assumed that the best styles of leadership could be learned.

The behavioral theories first divided leaders in two categories. Those that were concerned with the tasks and those concerned with the people. Throughout the literature these are referred to as different names, but the essence are identical.

Ohio State and University of Michigan

Studies conducted at the Ohio State University and the University of Michigan identified two leadership styles and two types of leader behaviors. The Ohio State study identified two leadership styles: considerate and initiating structure. The University of Michigan study classified leaders' behaviors as being employee-centered and production-centered.

The primary concern of leaders with considerate and employee-centered style is the employee's welfare. The primary concern of leaders with initiating-structure and production-centered styles is achieving goals. Research findings on which dimension is most important for satisfaction and productivity are inconclusive. However, employee-oriented considerate leaders appear to be associated with high group productivity and job satisfaction.

The Managerial Grid

The dimensions identified at the University of Michigan provided the basis for the development of the managerial grid model developed by Robert Blake and Jane Mouton. It identifies five various leadership styles that represent different combinations of concern for people and concern for production. Managers who scored high on both these dimensions simultaneously (labeled team management) performed best.

The five leadership styles of the managerial grid include impoverished, country club, produce or perish, middle-of-the road, and team. The impoverished style is located at the lower left-hand corner of the grid, point (1, 1). It is characterized by low concern for both people and production. The primary objective of the impoverished style is for managers to stay out of trouble. The country club style is located at the upper left–hand corner of the grid, point(1, 9). It is characterized as a high concern for people and a low concern for production. The primary objective of the country club style is to create a secure and comfortable atmosphere and trust that subordinates will respond positively. The produce or perish style is located at the lower right–hand corner of the grid, point(9, 1). A high concern for production and a low concern for people characterize it. The primary objective of the produce or perish style is to achieve the organization's goals. To accomplish the organization's goals, it is not necessary to consider employees' needs as relevant. The middle–of–the–road style is located at the middle of the grid, point(5, 5). A balance between workers' needs and the organization's productivity goals characterize it. The primary objective of the middle–of–the–road style is to maintain employee morale at a level sufficient to get the organization's work done. The team style is located at the upper right–hand of the grid, point(9, 9). It is characterized by a high concern for people and

Figure 3–6 Leadership Types of Managerial Grid

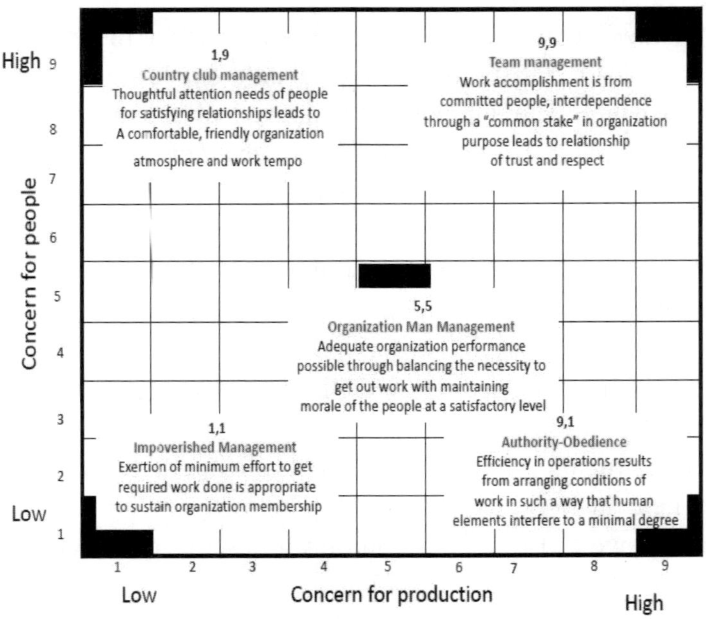

Source: http://4.bp.blogspot.com/-oTErh0jrJSM/UcKLCtam-ol/AAAAAAAAEZ4/7vty4JFrh-w/s1600/ManagerialGrid.JPG

production. The primary objective of the team style is to establish cohesion and foster a feeling of commitment among workers.

Contingency Theories

The contingency leadership theory argues that there is no single way of leading and that every leadership style should be based on certain situations.

Successful leaders must be able to adapt their leader behavior to meet the needs of their followers and of the particular situation. Even with good diagnostic skills, leaders may not be effective unless they can adapt their leadership style to meet the demands of their environment.

Fiedler's Contingency Model

Leadership Theory and Research: Perspectives and Directions(Academic Press Inc(HBJ), 1993) was a tribute to Fred Fiedler's 40 year study of leadership and organizational effectiveness. The contribution made by Fiedler is the realization that leadership effectiveness depends on the situations, and another contribution is the fact that he made the simplistic "one best way" approach of earlier eras obsolete.

Fred E. Fiedler's contingency theory postulates that there is no best way for managers to lead. Situations will create different leadership style requirements for a manager. The solution to a managerial situation is contingent on the factors that impinge on the situation. For example, in a highly routinized (mechanistic) environment where repetitive tasks are the norm, a certain leadership style may result in the best performance. The same leadership style may not work in a very dynamic environment.

Fiedler looked at three situations that could define the condition of a managerial task:

1. Leader member relations: How well do the manager and the employees get along?
2. The task structure: Is the job highly structured, fairly unstructured, or somewhere in between?
3. Position power: How much authority does the manager possess?

Managers were rated as to whether they were relationship oriented or task oriented. Task oriented managers tend to do better in situations that have good leader–member relationships, structured tasks, and either weak or strong position power.

They do well when the task is unstructured but position power is strong. Also, they did well at the other end of the spectrum when the leader member relations were moderate to poor and the task was unstructured.

Relationship oriented managers do better in all other situations. Thus, a given situation might call for a manager with a different style or a manager who could take on a different style for a different situation.

These environmental variables are combined in a weighted sum that is termed "Favorable" at one end and "unfavorable" at the other. Task oriented style is preferable at the clearly defined extremes of "favorable" and "unfavorable" environments, but relationship orientation excels in the middle ground. Managers could attempt to reshape the environment variables to match their style.

Figure 3–7 Fiedler's Contingency Model

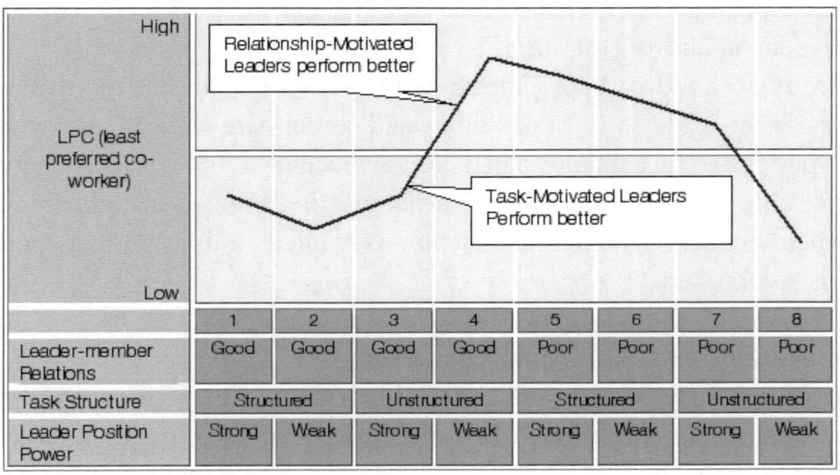

Source: https://images.search.yahoo.com/search/images?p=fiedler%26%2339%3Bs+contingency+model+of+leadership+picture&fr=yfp-t&imgurl=http%3A%2F%2Fwww.swlearning.com%2Fmanagement%2Fpierce%2Fmanagement3e%2Fpowerpoint%2Fch11%2Fimg022.gif#id=18&iurl=http%3A%2F%2Fi361.photobucket.com%2Falbums%2Fab177%2Fmorethanomm%2Ffor%2520omm%2520blog%2FFieldermodel.jpg&action=click

Another aspect of the contingency model theory is that the leader–member relations, task structure, and position power dictate a leader's situational control. Leader–member relations are the amount of loyalty, dependability, and support that the leader receives from employees. It is a measure of how the manager perceives he or she and the group of employees is getting along together.

In a favorable relationship the manager has a high task structure and is able to reward and or punish employees without any problems. In an unfavorable relationship the task is usually unstructured and the leader possesses limited authority. The spelling out in detail (favorable) of what is required of subordinates affects task structure.

Positioning power measures the amount of power or authority the manager perceives the organization has given him or her for the purpose of directing, rewarding, and punishing subordinates. Positioning power of managers depends on the taking away (favorable) or increasing (unfavorable) the decision–making power of employees.

The task–motivated style leader experiences pride and satisfaction in the task accomplishment for the organization, while the relationship–motivated style seeks to build interpersonal relations and extend extra help for the team development in the organization.

There is no good or bad leadership style. Each person has his or her own preferences for leadership. Task–motivated leaders are at their best when the group performs successfully such as achieving a new sales record or outperforming the major competitor. Relationship–oriented leaders are at their best when greater customer satisfaction is gained and a positive company image is established.

Hersey-Blanchard Situational Leadership

The Hersey–Blanchard Situational Leadership theory is based on the amount of direction (task behavior) and amount of socio–emotional support (relationship behavior) a leader must provide given the situation and the "level of maturity" of the followers.

Task behavior is the extent to which the leader engages in spelling out the duties and responsibilities to an individual or group. This behavior includes telling people what to do, how to do it, when to do it, where to do it, and who's to do it. In task behavior the leader engages in one–way communication.

Relationship behavior is the extent to which the leader engages in two-way or multi-way communications. This includes listening, facilitating, and supportive behaviors. In relationship behavior the leader engages in two-way communication by providing socio-emotional support.

Maturity is the willingness and ability of a person to take responsibility for directing his or her own behavior. People tend to have varying degrees of maturity, depending on the specific task, function, or objective that a leader is attempting to accomplish through their efforts.

To determine the appropriate leadership style to use in a given situation, the leader must first determine the maturity level of the followers in relation to the specific task that the leader is attempting to accomplish through the effort of the followers.

As the level of followers' maturity increases, the leader should begin to reduce his or her task behavior and increase relationship behavior until the followers reach a moderate level of maturity. As the followers begin to move into an above average level of maturity, the leader should decrease not only task behavior but also relationship behavior.

Figure 3-8 Hersey-Blanchard Situational Leadership

Source: http://www.drypen.in/human-resource/hersey-blanchard-situational-leadership-theory.html

Once the maturity level is identified, the appropriate leadership style can be determined. The four leadership styles are telling, selling, participating, and delegating.

High task/low relationship behavior(S1) is referred to as "telling." The leader provides clear instructions and specific direction. Telling style is best matched with a low follower readiness level. High task/high relationship behavior(S2) is referred to as "selling." The leader encourages two-way communication and helps build confidence and motivation on the part of the employee, although the leader still has responsibility and controls decision making. Selling style is best matched with a moderate follower readiness level.

High relationship/low task behavior(S3) is referred to as "participating." With this style, the leader and followers share decision making and no longer need or expect the relationship to be directive. Participating style is best matched with a moderate follower readiness level. Low relationship/low task behavior(S4) is labeled "delegating." This style is appropriate for leaders whose followers are ready to accomplish a particular task and are both competent and motivated to take full responsibility. Delegating style is best matched with a high follower readiness level.

2. Open System Theory: Structural Contingency Theory

In case of closed system theory, attention has been paid only to individuals and small groups in an organization, not the situational factors such as technology, job uncertainty, environment, size, goal and power. Open system is the dominant image in systems theory. Most of the organizational literature make an analogy of organizations as biological organism, and emphasize system survival, that is, maintenance of homeostasis through feedback (correcting deviation from equilibrium state) rather than internal efficiency. This view focuses on the relationship between a system and environment.

It seems logical that "one best way" is feasible, assuming that all organizations are alike. But assuming that organizations are faced with different situations, we need a different theory, which is contingency theory. Structural Contingency Theory(SCT) posits that the most appropriate form of organization depends not on one best way but on situational contingencies with which an organization is faced.

According to Burns and Stalker, rational configuration of an organization can be either mechanistic or organismic. The question of which form is more rational relies on such situational factors as job uncertainty. For example, Lawrence and Lorsch suggest that various types of structure should be designed within an organization. Because an organization may be confronted with various sub-environments.

Most modern theories on organization and environment presumes that organizational effectiveness can be improved by sustaining the fit between organization and environment. Structural Contingency Theory representing a system-structural view focuses on the fit between organization and technical environment. Equifinality principle that there can be many means to reach a final state is fundamentally different from that of causality or Taylor's one best way.

Figure 3-9 Organizational System in terms of Systems Theory

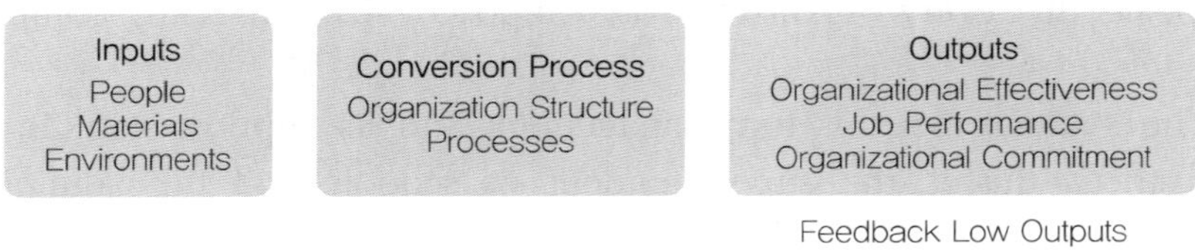

Thinking of the principle of requisite variety that internal structure of a system must be as various as complex environments a system is faced, one best way never exists from the systems theory view. Instead, various types of structure should be designed within an organization, because an organization may be confronted with various sub-environments.

Several theories above-mentioned view changes emerging from external environments gradually, and this gradual environmental changes can be coped with by organizations.

Population ecology theory insists that the adaptive capacity of an organization to environmental changes might be reduced once system equilibrium is maintained. Therefore organizational changes can be said to be a Darwinian selection rather than Lamarckian adaptation.

Darwinian selection and Larmarkian adaptation view among Quadrants I to IV in the previous <Table 3-1> consider conflicts as system-destructive and thus something to be alleviated, while dialectical analysis in Q IV and theories in Q V and VI consider conflicts as natural phenomena and thus doing developmental functions.

Quadrants V and VI show a totally different views on the locus of organizational changes from those of existing OT. The assumption that an organization adapts to environments passively, or enacts them actively, or interacts with them makes sense only in cases of Newtonian mechanical paradigm positing order in the orderliness and simplistic view on the universe and equilibrium model positing negative entropy.

However equilibrium model is being challenged by the concept of entropy. In case of nonequilibrium model where unanalysability of environments or order out of chaos is assumed, these assumptions are questioned.

Henry Mintzberg should be mentioned, since he epitomized the structural contingency very nicely. He introduces his five types of organizational structure and how they influence the functioning of organizations.

He posits that every organization is composed of the five key components.

- The strategic apex is top management and its support staff. In school districts, this is the superintendent of schools and the administrative cabinet.
- The operative core are the workers who actually carry out the organization's tasks. Teachers constitute the operative core in school districts.
- The middle line is middle—and lower—level management. Principals are the middle-level managers in school districts.
- The technostructure are analysts such as engineers, accountants, planners, researchers, and personnel managers. In school districts, divisions such as instruction, business, personnel, public relations, research and development, and the like constitute the technostructure.
- The support staff are the people who provide indirect services. In school districts, similar services include maintenance, clerical, food service, busing, legal counsel, and consulting to provide support.

Figure 3–10 The Key Parts of an Organization

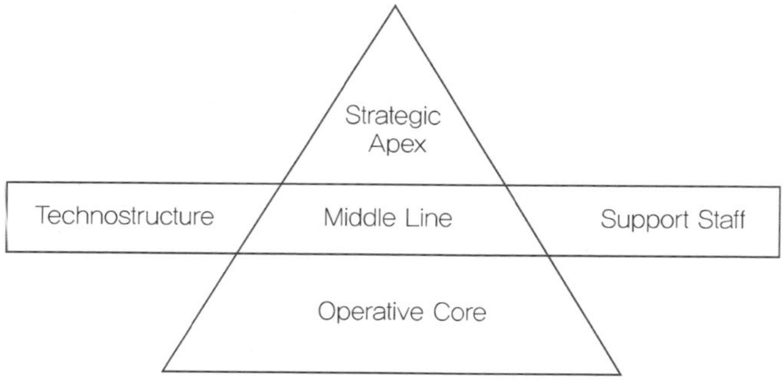

All organizations are made up of 5 basic parts; that is strategic apex(top mgt.), middle line, techno–structure, support staff, and operating core(street–level bureaucrats).

The combination of these components build five configurations of organizational; that is, simple structure, machine bureaucracy, professional bureaucracy, divisionalized form and adhocracy. Next each of the five structural configurations are summarized. And each organizational form is discussed in turn.

Table 3–3 Mintzberg's Five Organizational Structures

Structural Configuration	Prime Coordinating Mechanism	Key Part of Organization	Type of Decentralization
Simple structure	Direct supervision	Strategic apex	Vertical and horizontal centralization
Machine bureaucracy	Standardization of work processes	Technostructure	Limited horizontal decentralization
Professional bureaucracy	Standardization of skills	Operating core	Vertical and horizontal decentralization
Divisionalized form	Standardization of outputs	Middle line	Limited vertical decentralization
Adhocracy	Mutual adjustment	Support staff	Selective decentralization

Source: Mintzberg, H.(1992). *Structure in fives: Designing effective organizations*. Upper Saddle River, N.J.: Prentice Hall.

Simple Structure

Also called the entrepreneurial organization, the simple structure is a vertically organized pyramid with vertical lines of authority. Its key characteristics are direct supervision of subordinates, organic organization according to functions and a lack of formal support structures. Authority is concentrated at the peak in the person of the CEO. Small and young organizations often fall into this category because it is the default structure that develops when the entrepreneur avoids formal restrictions.

Figure 3–11 Simple Structure

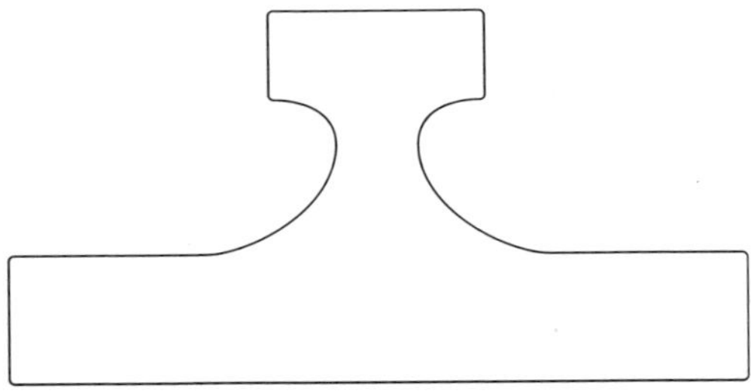

Machine Bureaucracy

The machine bureaucracy gets its name from its high level of work standardization, making organizational units function together like the parts of a machine. Companies with mass–produced output use this form. Tasks are standardized and detailed in operating procedures that allow employees to carry out their work with a minimum of training. Lines of authority are formal, with some power residing in the groups that develop the policies and procedures that govern the company.

Figure 3–12 Machine Bureaucracy

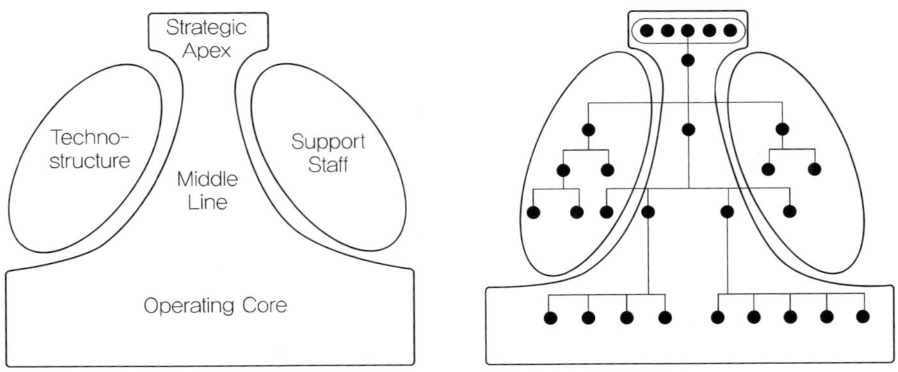

Professional Bureaucracy

The professional bureaucracy is bureaucratic without being centralized. It relies on highly qualified professionals to carry out the work with a high degree of independence. The organization achieves its coordination of functions by standardizing the skills and qualifications required to carry out the work of a particular position.

The bureaucracy focuses on defining positions in terms of capabilities and making sure these mesh to allow the organization to function.

Figure 3–13 Professional Bureaucracy

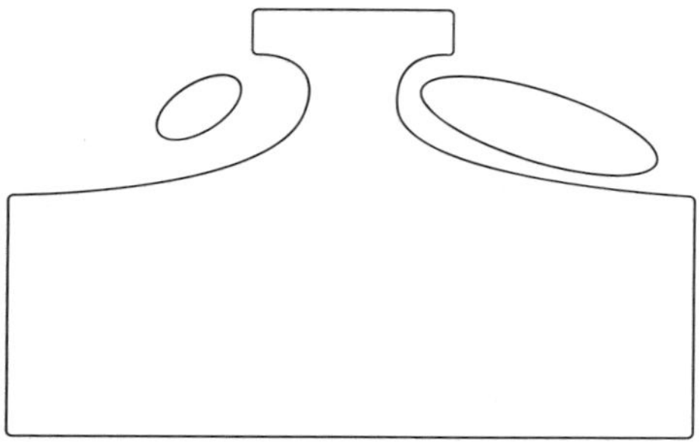

Divisionalized Form

Large organizations with diversified products create divisions to handle related activities. The advantage of this divisionalized organizational structure is that the divisions can act with a high degree of autonomy to address their particular situations, while the central part of the organization concentrates on

Figure 3–14 Divisionalized Form

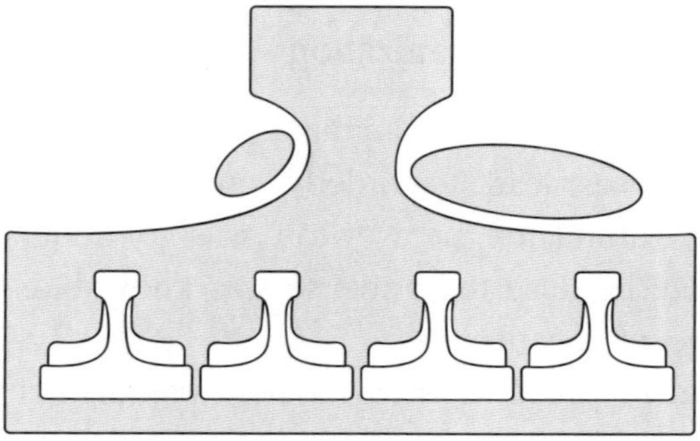

the big picture.

The existence of divisions also means that there is an inherent duplication of activities, with each division containing essential functions such as sales, human resources and accounting.

Adhocracy

Formal organizational structures take time to adjust to changes. In industries that are changing rapidly or in project-based companies where projects are all different, such formal structures limit the required flexibility. The adhocracy adapts to whatever situation it encounters.

Its characteristics include a lack of formal structure combined with a variety of highly skilled employees. The adhocracy forms teams to carry out work. Teams are self-organizing with matrix structures that allow effective vertical and horizontal sharing of authority based on competence and the particular situation.

Figure 3-15 Adhocracy; A Temporary Committee

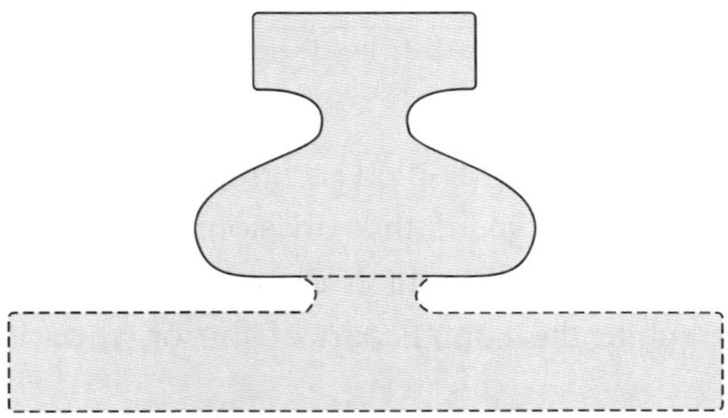

3. Chaos Theory: Self-Organization

Historically, the classical world paradigm describes a deterministic universe in which orderly causes lead to orderly outcomes. The ultimate goal of classical science as formulated by Newton was to understand the universe, which could be done because the universe was knowable. Recently, there has been radical change of perspective.

From the natural to social sciences, a new paradigm has emerged where instabilities, fluctuations, or chaos describe the underlying condition of the universe, rather than order. This paradigm suggests that order emerges from instabilities. The paradigm shifts understanding from a classically mechanistic view to a one of a world of systems.

Composed of complex and paradoxical elements. From this perspective, orderly systems must themselves be described by complexity and paradox in order to cope with the chaos they have to cope with(Prigogine, 1980, 1996). The scientific formulation of chaos originated in the study of dynamic systems.

Recent developments associated with chaos have opened new roads of investigation for organizational researchers to deal with the dilemma of determinism, the position of man and institutions in nature from this new light (Prigogine, 1996).

The purpose is to suggest ways of operationalizing characteristics of organizations from this perspective and then investigate ways of increasing organizational member commitment to the implications of such systems.

Chaos is not anarchy. It has two characteristics. At one level it is inherently unpredictable and at another level it displays a hidden pattern(Stacy, 1992: 62). Hence chaos consists of a combination of order and disorder, regularity and irregularity, in which pattern unfold in irregular but similar forms.

Patterns of behavior which are irregular but are nevertheless recognizable as broad categories of behavior, or archetypes, within which there is endless individual variety(Stacey, 1992).

Non-linear systems produce synergistic behaviors among their components when people in the system have a holistic or systemic perspective for understanding the system.

The potential for confusion on the part of organizational members exists due to short term fluctuations and change which may appear random and without meaning.

It is only when the larger patterns are understood that short term instabilities have a context. Thus, chaos is not random, unstable behavior because it's instability is bounded and has an overall pattern.

Researchers of chaos theories are discovering that creative, innovative systems can cope with environmental instabilities far better than traditional systems. Systems that are continually creative and innovative are also called far-from-equilibrium systems since they seem to operate with continual experimentation and restructuring.

From this perspective, chaos, instability, and fluctuation cause innovation and evolution of a system only if that instability(Prigogine, 1980; Nicolis & Prigogine, 1989; Prigogine & Stengers, 1984; Prigogine, Nicolis & Babloyantz, 1972).

A number of organizational theorists have discussed the implications of this new conceptual framework(Thietart & Forgues, 1995, 1997; Begum, 1994; Smith & Comer, 1994; Smith & Gemmill, 1991). Traditional management, based on the goal of stable equilibrium, tend to damp and constrain change.

In contrast, systems based on chaos and dynamic systems tend to encourage and reinforce change to increase complexity. These types of systems have the capability of importing energy or information from the environment which is then utilized or dissipated through the system while still preserving structure.

These so called dissipative structures are capable of renewing themselves spontaneously by producing more complex and qualitatively different forms of structure through a process of self-organization(Prigogine, 1980; Prigogine & Stengers, 1984).

Organizational change becomes the essence of organizational functioning in contrast to the traditional management theories' focus on control in order to maintain organizational order keeping internal and external equilibria.

Ralph Stacey created something similar, called the Agreement & Certainty Matrix. It shows Simple, Complicated, Complex, and Anarchy (Chaos) as four

Figure 3-16 Agreement & Certainty Matrix

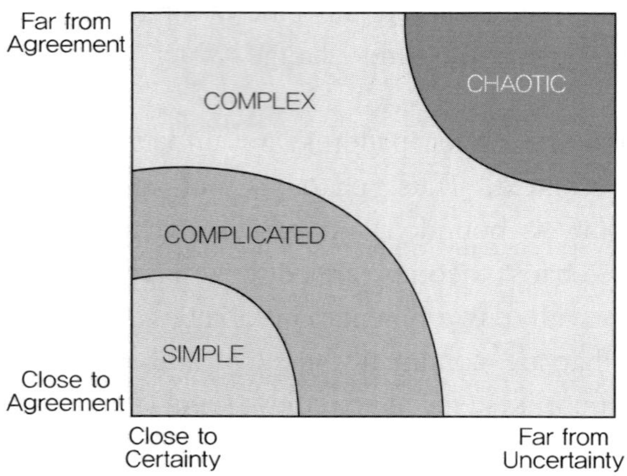

areas based in two dimensions: the degree of agreement and the degree of uncertainty. And he further argues that traditional social sciences have mainly focused on the simple and complicated areas only. On the other hand, complexity theory including chaos theory expands the sphere to complex area.

This idea can be applied to various fields for approaching complex situations in not only decision–making but also public management and policy settings. It can help to guide you by offering an additional method to select the appropriate management actions in a complex adaptive system (CAS) based on two axes:

There is a large area on this diagram which lies between the anarchy/chaos region (4) and regions of the traditional management approaches (1, 2 & 3). Stacey calls this large center region the zone of complexity (5) others call it the edge of chaos. In the zone of complexity the traditional management approaches are not very effective but it is the zone of high creativity, innovation, and breaking with the past to create new modes of operating.

Figure 3–17 The Edge of Chaos(The Zone of Complexity)

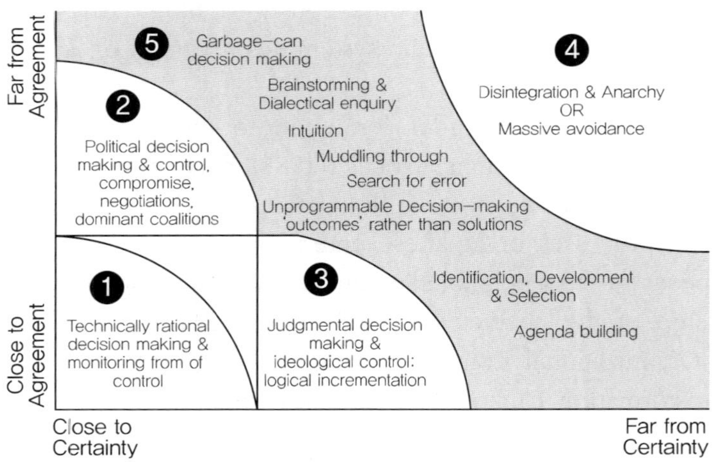

Sources: Stacey, Ralph(1992). *Managing the Unknowable: The Strategic Boundaries Between Order and Chaos*.

This interest in organizational transformation or self–renewing systems comes at a time when global competition among companies and environ–

mental change require employee creativity and innovativeness. The theory of complex nonlinear, self-organizing systems serves as a general framework (Nicolis, 1977; Prigogine, 1980; Allen, 1984; Laszlo, 1987).

Some theorists in organization studies discuss a dissipative structure model of organizational transformation and the system processes essential for such a system to become and maintain itself as a dissipative structure(Gemmill & Smith, 1985; Leifer, 1989; Malaska, 1991). Although they identify certain or components of system transformation within the self-organizing paradigm, they have not operationalized the characteristics of self-organizing paradigm, they have not operationalized the characteristics of self-organizing systems in a work context(Nonaka, 1988).

After reviewing relevant studies, Nonaka(1988) described the process of creating a new order as follows;

In a system condition, an element fluctuates. It acts on the neighboring elements one after another, and the fluctuation begins to be amplified, which is called butterfly effect or the sensitivity to initial conditions. When a macroscopic pattern emerges from such a dynamic cooperative phenomenon, a feedback to each element take place, reinforcing the dynamic cooperation. Thus, a definite order is formed spontaneously forming a stable order. When the order becomes fixed, the organic system again carries on a similar process irreversibly.

Applying this process of order formation to the process of creation of information within organizations, Nonaka(1985) conceptualized characteristics of self-organizing systems in a work context based on observations of the self-renewing processes of Japanese enterprises.

The purpose was to operationalize and explore the (SOS), and to examine the relationship of the characteristics of Self-Organizing Systems(SOS) with employees' Organizational Commitment(OC).

Since transformation can only be as successful as employees commitment to it, we focus on conditions that lead to increasing commitment. In contrast to most of the research on self organizing systems that focus at a theoretical, or at best a management perspective, this study investigates the relationships between self-organizing systems and their effects on employees' organizational commitment, loyalty, and feelings of attachment to the goals and values of the organization.

Table 3-4 Key Scholars in OT

Classical Organization Theory	Fayol(1949). *General Principles of Management in General and Industrial Management.* Taylor(1916). *Principles of Scientific Management in Bulletin of the Taylor Society.* Weber(1946). Bureaucracy in Essays in Sociology. Gulick(1937). Papers on the Science of Administration.
Neo-classical Organization Theory	Barnard(1966). *The Functions of the Executive.* Merton(1957). *Social Theory and Social Structure.* Simon(1946). Proverbs of Administration. *PAR 6.*
Modern Structural Organization Theory	Burns & Stalker(1961). The Management of Innovation. Blau & Scott(1962). *Formal Organizations.* Walker & Lorch(1968). Organizational Choice: Product versus Function. *Harvard Business Review.* Nov. Mintzberg(1979). *The Structure of Organizations.* Jaques(1990). In Praise of Hierarchy. *Harvard Business Review.* Jan.
Human Resource Theory, or the Organizational Behavior Perspective	Follet(1926). Scientific Foundations of Business Administration. Roethlisberger(1941). *Management and Morale.* Maslow(1943). A Theory of Human Motivation. *Psychological Review.* 50. McGregor(1957). The Human Side of Enterprise.
Systems Theory and Organizational Economics	Katz & Kahn(1966). *The Social Psychology of Organizations.* Thompson(1967). *Organizations in Action.*

References

Heffron, Florence(1989). *Organization Theory and Public Organizations: The Political Connection.*

Miller, D., & Droge, C.(1986). Psychological and Traditional Determinants of Structure. *Administrative Science Quarterly*, 31: 539－560.

Mintzberg, H.(1979). *The Structure of Organizations.* Englewood Cliffs, N.J.: Prentice－Hall.

______(1983). *Structure in Fives: Designing Effective Organizations.* Englewood Cliffs, N.J.: Prentice－Hall, Inc.

Morgan, Gareth(1986). *Images of Organization*, SAGE Publications Inc.: Calif.

Pfeffer, Jeffrey(1982). *Organizations and Organization Theory.* Boston: Pitman.

Stacey, Ralph(1992). *Managing the Unknowable: The Strategic Boundaries Between Order and Chaos.* Jossey Bass, San Francisco.

Taylor, Frederick W.(1967). *The Principles of Scientific Management.* New York: W. W. Norton & Company.

Thompson, James D.(1967). *Organizations in Action.* New York: McGraw－Hill.

Weber, Max(1947). *The Theory of Social and Economic Organization.* trans, A. M. Parsons & T. Parsons, New York Free Press.

Weick, Karl(1979). *The Social Psychology of Organizing.* 2nd ed., Reading, Mass. Addison Wesley Publishing Co.

Part 2. Organization Theory Cases

1. Morgan discusses organizations metaphorically in an attempt to explain them more fully. Try to explain an organization as metaphors.

2. Watch football games and try to understand the organizing principles of soccer teams.

   2-1) How are organizing principles of classical OT and bureaucratic theory represented in soccer teams?

   2-2) How can you apply 4 mgt principles of Taylor's Scientific Management to soccer teams?

   2-3) How do you think Hiddink applied Taylor's Scientific Management to soccer teams?

3. Watch the first 15 minutes of the movie Modern Times by Charlie Chaplin, and answer the following questions.

   3-1) What do you think is the main theme of this movie?

   3-2) What are organizing principles in Modern Times?

   3-3) What lessons did the modern organizations learn from this movie?

4. Describe the streams of organization theories.
5. Compare such content motivation theories as Maslow, Alderfer, Hertzberg.
6. Compare behavioral approaches to leadership theories such as Univ. of Michgan, Ohio State Univ. and Managerial Grid theory.
7. Explain the five structures of Mintzberg.
8. Explain the images of organization of Gareth Morgan.
9. Surf the Internet and try to find out the process theory of motivation such as expectancy theory and goal-setting theory.
10. Explain agreement and certainty matrix by Stacey.

Class Exercise

The Large Consequences of Small Courses

1) "*For the want of a nail the shoe was lost,*
For the want of a shoe the horse was lost,
For the want of a horse the rider was lost,
For the want of a rider the battle was lost,
For the want of a battle the kingdom was lost,
And all for the want of a horseshoe–nail."
Benjamin Franklin
Poor Richard's Almanac, 1758

2) The Butterfly Effect
James Gleick
Chaos: Making a New Science, 1987

Using Benjamin Franklin's well–known poem (above) and Gleick's concept of the Butterfly Effect explain:

1. The basic tenets of systems organization theory.
2. The modern organization as an "organic" system.
3. How does technology have a systems impact on the modern organization?
4. How does a more educated workforce have a systems impact on the modern organization?
5. How can leadership affect "dynamic equilibrium" in the organizational system?

Part 3 Public Policy

Honesty is always the best policy in the end.

—Gerald R. Ford

01
Chapter

The Definition and Process of Public Policy

I never had a policy; I have just tried to do my very best each and every day.

—Abraham Lincoln

LEARNING OBJECTIVES

After reading Chapter 1, the student should be able to:

1. Understand the definition of public policy.
2. Understand the process of public policy.
3. Understand the policy-making models such as rational-comprehensive, incremental, satisficing, and garbage can models.

1. The Definition of Public Policy

Public policy is an attempt by a government to address a public issue by instituting laws, regulations, decisions, or actions relevant to the problem at hand. Numerous issues can be addressed by public policy including crime, education, foreign policy, health, and social welfare.

The process to create a new public policy typically follows three steps: agenda-setting, option-formulation, and implementation; the time-line for a new policy to be put in place can range from weeks to several years, depending on the situation. Public policies can also be made by leaders of religious and cultural institutions for the benefit of the congregation and participants, and the term can also refer to a type of academic study that covers topics such as sociology, economics, and policy analysis.

2. The Process of Public Policy

When new public policies are created, there are generally three key things involved in the process: the problem, the player, and the policy. The problem is the issue that needs to be addressed, the player is the individual or group that is influential in forming a plan to address the problem in question, and the policy is the finalized course of action decided upon by the government.

Typically the general public will make the government aware of an issue through writing letters and emails, or making phone calls, to local government leaders; the issue is then brought forward during government meetings and the process for creating new public policies begins.

The rational model for the public policy-making process can typically be divided into three steps: agenda-setting, option-formulation, and implementation. Within the agenda-setting stage, the agencies and government officials meet to discuss the problem at hand.

In the second stage, option-formulation, alternative solutions are considered and final decisions are made regarding the best policy. Consequently, the decided policy is implemented during the final stage; in most cases, once public policies are in place, they are widely open to interpretation by non-governmental players, including those in the private sector.

Implied within this model is the fact that the needs of the society are a priority for the players involved in the policy-making process; also, it is believed that the government will follow through on all decisions made by the final policy.

Unfortunately, those who frame the issue to be addressed by policy often exert an enormous amount of influence over the entire process through their personalities, personal interests, political affiliations, and so on. The bias is extenuated by the players involved.

The final outcome of the process, as well as its implementation, is therefore not as effective as what could result from a purely rational process. Overall, however, public policy continues to be a vital tool in addressing social concerns.

Examples

In 1993, due to ineffective healthcare policies, the Clinton administration in the US sought to implement a policy that would bring about a national healthcare system. As part of the policies being considered, the US federal government would protect the healthcare consumer's rights, consumers would be able to form alliances to obtain better healthcare prices, and care givers would be required to provide fair healthcare packages.

Players involved in the policy-making process included lobbying groups and politicians. While some changes were made to healthcare provisions by legislators, the policies advocated by the Clinton administration were not put into effect as result of political differences.

In 2010, US president Barack Obama signed the Affordable Care Act into law; this health care reform and public policy is meant to offer all American citizens health insurance that is easier to afford. The policy implemented several changes in health care that no longer allow health insurance companies to deny coverage to children with pre-existing conditions, nor can they drop coverage when insurance carriers become ill.

Making public policy is extraordinarily complex. It involves public opinion, media attitudes, expert ideas, active citizens, business and labor leaders, elected representatives, presidents and governors, judges, and bureaucrats.

Policymaking calls on political resources, economic conditions, popular cultural attitudes, and international conditions. When political scientists do research attempting to understand public policy, they try to reduce the complexity of the policy making process to a manageable degree by creating models of policy making that summarize the primary forces at work.

The idea of modeling the policy process in terms of stages was first put forward by Lasswell. As part of his attempt to establish a multidisciplinary and prescriptive policy science, Lasswell introduced in 1956 a model of the policy process comprised of seven stages: intelligence, promotion, prescription, invocation, application, termination, and appraisal.

While this sequence of stages has been contested, the model itself has been highly successful as a basic framework for the field of policy studies and became the starting point of a variety of typology of the policy process. Based on the growth of the field of policy studies during the 1960s and 1970s, the stages models served the basic need to organize and systemize a growing body of literature and research.

Figure 1–1 Stages of Policy–making Processes

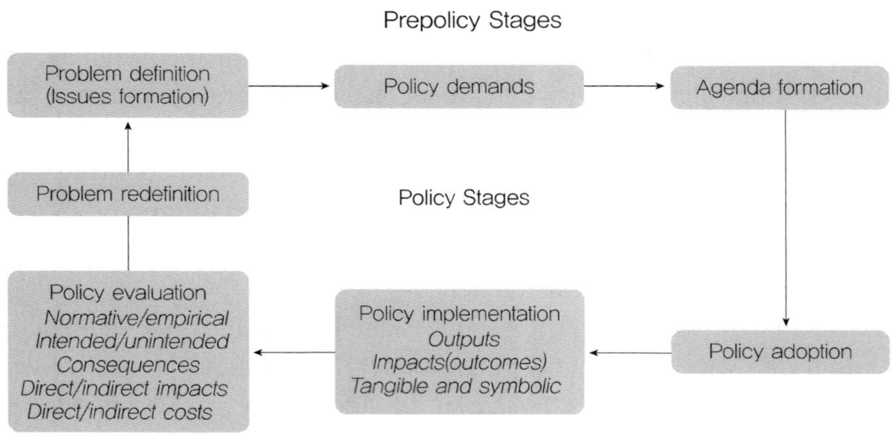

Source: Clark, Cochran E., et. al.(2009). *American Public Policy*, Wadsworth Pub. Co.

1) Agenda Formation

Before a policy can be created, a problem must exist that is called to the attention of the government. Agenda formation or agenda setting is the creation of public awareness and concern of salient issues by the news media; two basic assumptions underlie on agenda setting: 1) the press and the media do reflect reality, they filter and shape it, and 2) media concentration on a few issues and subjects leads the public to perceive those issues as more important than other issues(X1, X4, and X6).

And these issues become public issues, politics issues and finally policy issues such as security issues due to frequent crime accidents.

Figure 1–2 Agenda Issue Formation

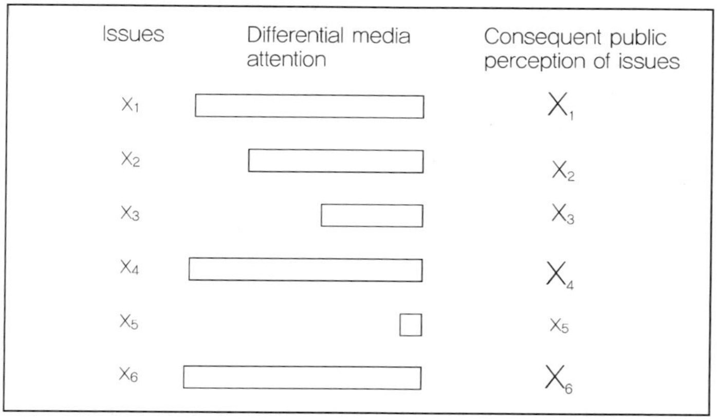

Source: http://sonamjourno.blogspot.kr/2011/03/agenda-setting-theory.html

Illegal immigration, for example, has been going on for many years, but it was not until the 1990s that enough people considered it such a serious problem that it required increased government action.

Another example is crime. American society tolerates a certain level of crime; however, when crime rises dramatically or is perceived to be rising dramatically, it becomes an issue for policy makers to address.

Specific events can place a problem on the agenda. The flooding of a town near a river raises the question of whether homes should be allowed to be built in a floodplain. New legislation on combating terrorism (the USA Patriot Act, for example) was a response to the attacks of September 11, 2001.

2) Policy Adoption and Policy–making

Policy formulation means coming up with an approach to solving a problem. Congress, the executive branch, the courts, and interest groups may be involved. Contradictory proposals are often made. the police may adopt "War against Crime" policy and program. The president may have one approach to immigration reform, and the opposition–party members of Congress may have another. Policy formulation has a tangible outcome: A bill goes before Congress or a regulatory agency drafts proposed rules. The process continues with adoption. A policy is adopted when Congress passes legislation, the regulations become final, or the Supreme Court renders a decision in a case.

Important policy-making models are rational-comprehensive, incremental, satisficing, and garbage can models.

(1) Rational-comprehensive Model

The rational-comprehensive theory is a very well thought-out, step-by-step map to making good public policy decisions. The steps involved in this theory are(real life application example of this model): [1] identify the problem and define it(to buy or not to buy a notebook); [2] decide on the goals to be reached to solve the problem(to buy the cheapest one or to buy the best one); [3] identify all of the alternatives and to reaching this goal(notebooks in mind such as Samsung, LG, HP, Apple McBook, to name just a few); [4] evaluate the consequences of each of the alternatives based on criteria to evaluate these options(price, weight, etc.); [5] compare the alternatives and their consequences and choose the one which best reaches the goal with the least adverse consequences(buy the notebook with the highest utility value).

Table 1-1 Example of Rational-comprehensive Model

Alternatives/ DM Criteria	Price	CPU	Ram	HD Capacity	Size	Weight	Criterion you add	Total Utility*
Samsung NB Notebook Sense NT370	8	6						
NT900	7	7						
P560	6	8						
LG NB XNote	7	8						
HP NB	8	9						
Apple McBook	5	7						
McBook Pro	4	8						

* Utility can range from any value to any value, for instance 1<=Utility<=10

As logical as the model sounds, it, too, has many problems. First, it assumes that there is the best way to solve a problem and that policy makers are able to define the problem. It also assumes that the goals of the policy are clear(the real problem is to delay buying the notebook rather than to buy or not to buy a notebook) before it is implemented.

When you cannot define the problem, it's hard to set goals to reach the resolution of the problem. This model also assumes that the policy makers can find out all the alternatives(imagine how many notebooks are on the market all over the world) and foresee the consequences of all the alternatives.

(2) Incremental Model

The near opposite of the rational–comprehensive theory is the incremental theory. This theory makes the opposite assumptions of the rational–comprehensive theory. Incrementalism assumes: [1] the goals are unclear; [2] the problem, goals and implementation are intertwined and will evolve; [3] alternatives and goals are formed as learned; [4] policy makers are not free to choose the best alternatives because they must consider the feasibility and acceptability of possible policies.

Maybe in real life, assume that we have Samsung NB Sense NT370 and we cannot afford to buy a much better one, and we will tend to be forced to choose Samsung NB Sense NT900 which a incrementally improved choice than the previous model.

An example of incrementalism often cited is the congressional budget decision–making in the U.S., where the usual questions considered about a given (existing) agency might typically range from whether to cut 4 or 5 percent from its budget to whether to tack on a 5 or 10% increase.

Congress very seldom stops to think seriously about whether the agency ought to be abolished entirely as unnecessary or harmful to the public interest or whether its responsibilities would be better performed in some entirely different manner by another agency.

Consequently, one of the best predictors of an agency's budget in a given year is that same agency's budget for the year before plus or minus a small increment representing the rate of growth or shrinkage of total government revenues rather than Zero–Based Budgeting(ZBB).

(3) Simon's Bounded Rationality and Satisficing Model

Simon speculates that policy makers (irrespective of their level of intelligence) have to work under three unavoidable constraints: (1) only limited, often unreliable, information is available regarding possible alternatives and their consequences(Can you think of every option possible? Could you possibly go to all the shops?), (2) human mind has only limited capacity to evaluate and process the information that is available(it's said that due to cognitive limits we cannot consider more than 5~7 criteria simultaneously), and (3) only a limited amount of time is available to make a decision(would you fly to America to search notebooks? will you spend 2 years to find out them? And some say that it's best to purchase electronic goods just before he or she die).

Therefore even individuals who intend to make rational choices are bound to make satisficing choices in complex situations. These limits (bounds) on rationality also make it nearly impossible to make maximizing or optimizing choices, necessitating reliance on rules of thumb.

And based on the premise that decision making is not rational, Simon argues that decision making is characterized by 1) limited information processing, 2) use of rules of thumb or shortcuts, and 3) satisficing(Simon, 1957; March, James G. & Simon, Herbert, 1958).

(4) Garbage Can Model

Organizations are characterized as garbage cans into which are dumped problems, people, choice situations, and solutions (See organizations for the resulting definition of organization. A crucial variable in this model is timing. It is assumed that there is a continual stream of participants(PARs), solutions (Ss), choice opportunities(COs), and problems(Ps) that flow in and out of an organization.

Every now and then some clusters of these elements coincide, and a decision is produced in such ways that resolution, oversight and flight is made. Three major decision strategies in a garbage can model are the strategies of resolution, oversight and flight.

Figure 1–3 Garbage Can Model

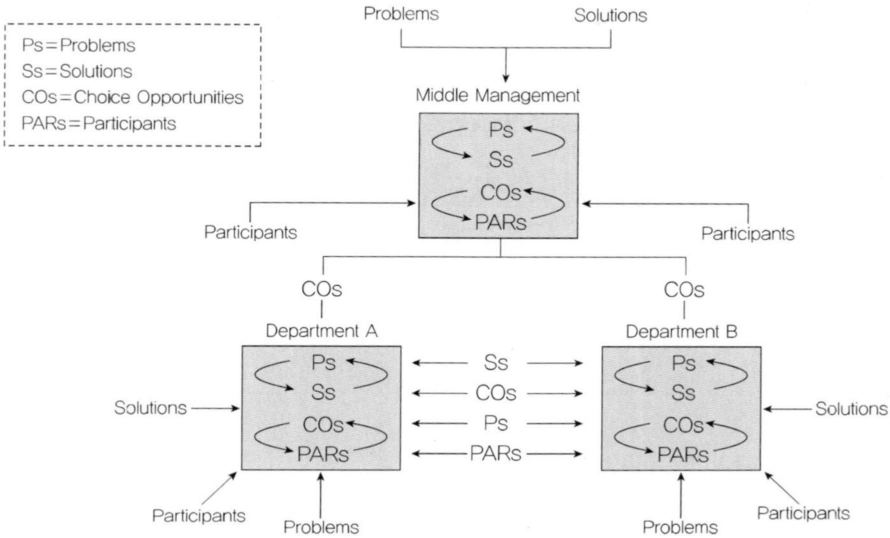

Source: Cohen, Michael D, James G. March, & Johan P, Olsen(1972). A Garbage Can Model of Organizational Choice Administrative Science Quarterly, 17(1).

Figure 1–4 Garbage Can

PARs: me, parents, brothers and sisters, friends, relatives
Ps: Buying Notebook
COs: Samsung NB Sense NT370, LG, HP, Apple McBook
Ss: Parents buy for me! I upgrade mine, I'll buy by working part–time, I just buy by careless instinct. My aunt happens to give his notebook to me, I decide to delay buying.

The strategy of resolution involves resolving(solving or deciding) problems after some period of working on them. The length of time may vary, depending on the number of problems. This is the familiar case that is implicit in most discussions of choice within organizations(I'll buy by working part–time for some period of time).

The strategy of oversight involves making quick choices. You make a choice whenever important problems are attached to some other choice(I just buy by careless instinct during my shopping). Likewise, the decision style of flight involves delaying or escaping from a choice until the problems wander away. Once the problems have left, then you make the choice. Again the choice solves no problems, since none are attached to it(I decide to delay buying).

Figure 1–5 Decision Strategies in a Garbage Can Model

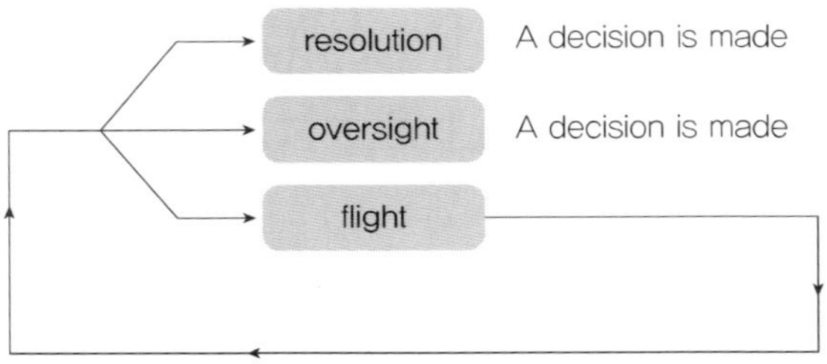

3) Policy Implementation

The implementation or carrying out of policy is most often accomplished by institutions other than those that formulated and adopted it. A statute usually provides just a broad outline of a policy. For example, Congress may mandate improved water quality standards, but the Environmental Protection Agency(EPA) provides the details on those standards and the procedures for measuring compliance through regulations.

An ideal process of policy implementation would include the following core elements:

- Specification of program details(i.e., how and by which agencies/organizations should the program be executed? How should the law and program be interpreted?);
- Allocation of resources(i.e., how are budgets distributed? Which personnel will execute the program? Which units of an organization will be in charge for the execution?);
- Decisions(i.e., how will decisions of single cases be carried out?)

4) Policy Evaluation and Termination

Evaluation means determining how well a policy is working, and it is not an easy task. People inside and outside of government typically use cost–benefit analysis to try to find the answer. In other words, if the government is spending x millions of dollars on this policy, are the benefits derived from it worth the expenditure? Cost–benefit analysis is based on data that are subject to different, and sometimes contradictory, interpretations.

History has shown that once implemented, policies are difficult to terminate. When they are terminated, it is usually because the policy became obsolete, clearly did not work, or lost its support among the interest groups and elected officials that placed it on the agenda in the first place.

In 1974, for example, Congress enacted a national speed limit of 55 miles per hour. It was effective in reducing highway fatalities and gasoline consumption. On the other hand, the law increased costs for the trucking industry and was widely viewed as an unwarranted federal intrusion into an area that belonged to the states to regulate. The law was abolished in 1987.

Overall, the analysis of the final stage of the policy cycle has witnessed a substantial departure from its initial focus(Fisher, Frank, et. al., 2007, *Handbook of Public Policy Analysis: Theory, Politics, and Method*. New York: CRC Press).

3. The Concepts in Public Policy

Complex social problems, such as crime, the economy, health care, and foreign policy, have multiple dimensions requiring multiple approaches. The various dimensions and the many policy initiatives required to address them mean that major public problems will never have single policy solutions.

There is no "one policy fits all for responding to terrorism," for example. Border security, electronic and human intelligence, military action, disaster preparedness, and many other initiatives are required.

This means as well that any major policy issue requires choices and trade–offs. There are limited resources of time, money, and attention. Spending more on border security may leave less for intelligence gathering, not to mention less for education or crime policy.

Outcome evaluations focus on the impact of the policy or program. Thus, outcome evaluation of a community policing policy would examine whether there was an impact on crime in the neighborhood, such as reduction in burglaries. Both forms of evaluation are necessary for a complete assessment of the policy.

Policies also have long–term effects and short–term impacts. Both need to be considered in evaluation. Similarly, some policies have symbolic importance. The decision to build a new football stadium for a professional team may have great symbolic importance to the residents of a city.

The stadium project may have been justified in part on the basis of making a world–class city and thus would be an intended symbolic benefit.

Costs and benefits of some programs are difficult to measure. How do we measure the benefit of clean air? Businesses may want to measure it in one way: the cost to them. Clean air advocates, however, may want to measure it in terms of the incidence of medical problems in the communities affected by the quality of the air near a manufacturing plant.

Table 1–2 Concepts in Policy Analysis

Concept	Definition	Examples
Agenda formation	The creation of public awareness and concern of salient issues	Security issue due to crime accidents
Policy Adoption & Policy–making	Coming up with an approach to solving a problem	War against Crime policy
Implementation	Steps taken to put a policy into practice	Hiring police; building prisons
Outputs	Measurable results of policy adoption and implementation	Numbers of police; conviction rates
Outcomes	Actual effects that policy outputs have on society	Crime rates; feelings of safety
Short–term Outcomes	Outcomes evaluated shortly after policy is implemented	Changes in crime rate during the year after a policy change
Long–term	Outcomes evaluated after policy has been in place for a longer time	Changes in crime rate over ten years
Policy evaluation	Process of assessing impacts of a policy	Assessment of effectiveness of a program intended to reduce crime rate
Cost–benefit analysis	Compares benefits of a program with costs of implementing it	Money spent; crime rate reduction

Source: Clark, Cochran E. et. al.(2009). *American Public Policy*. Wadsworth Pub. Co.

References

Clark, Cochran E. et. al.(2009). *American Public Policy*. Wadsworth Pub. Co.

Fischer, Frank, et. al., ed.(2007). *Handbook of Public Policy Analysis: Theory, Politics, and Method*. New York: CRC Press

March, James G. & Simon, Herbert(1958). *Organizations*. John Wiley and Sons. ISBN 0-471-56793-0.

Simon, Herbert(1957). "A Behavioral Model of Rational Choice." in Models of Man, Social and Rational: Mathematical Essays on Rational Human Behavior in a Social Setting. New York: Wiley.

02
Chapter

The Korean Public Policy

Surround yourself with the best people you can find, delegate authority, and don't interfere as long as the policy you've decided upon is being carried out.

— Ronald Reagan

LEARNING OBJECTIVES

After reading Chapter 2, the student should be able to:

1. Understand the public policy in The Chosun Dynasty and in the Military Government.
2. Understand the public policy in Korea.

1. Public Policy in The Chosun Dynasty and in the Military Government

The Chosun dynasty in the Korean peninsula from 1392 to 1910 was a society governed by the philosophy of Confucianism. Policy making during this period was made by kings and elites who were called Seonbi. The ideal Seonbi were leaders who possessed high moral character, extensive knowledge of philosophy, poetry, manners, and history. But there was nothing like a formal discipline that dealt with politics or policy during the Chosun dynasty.

The main guidance for statesmen was historical knowledge, stories that provided policy makers with some lessons relevant to the time. This remained the case until recent times when policy analysis as an academic field was introduced in Korea, largely taking its lead from American social science.

In the early 1960s, Korea was one of the poorest countries in the world and heavily dependent upon on aid from other countries. In 1961, a military coup took over the government and an Economic Planning Board was created as the most powerful planning and administration agency in Korea.

The military government announced a five-year plan of economic development, as it put a priority on economic development. The model put into place pursued rapid economic growth. Under the control of these political arrangements, citizens had no chance to participate in public policy making and implementation.

2. Public Policy in Korea

From now on we examine the history of Korean policy analysis from 1960s to the present in order to understand its development. One way to look at the evolution of policy analysis is by examining the nature and content of the articles published in the field. Toward this end, various Korean scholars have reviewed the policy articles that had been published in major Korean journals.

Kwon(1996) analyzed previous policy studies in Korean Public Administration Review(KPAR) from 1967 to 1995. According to him, 67 percent of those policy articles in KPAR applied a descriptive approach and 33 percent of them had a quantitative orientation.

Following Kwon, Hong & Kim(2001) analyzed 77 articles that addressed policy issues in KPAR from 1996 to 2001. According to them, while 23 percent were descriptive in nature, the other 77 percent involved explanatory studies that investigated the correlation between social and political factors(Fisher, Frank, et. al., 2007, *Handbook of Public Policy Analysis: Theory, Politics, and Method*. New York: CRC Press).

References

Clark, Cochran E. et. al.(2009). *American Public Policy.* Wadsworth Pub. Co.

Fischer, Frank, et. al., ed.(2007). *Handbook of Public Policy Analysis: Theory, Politics, and Method.* CRC Press.

Hong, S., & Kim, J.(2001). Research of policy science: Past, present, and future. A paper presented at a Conference of Korean Public Administration for 21st Century and Vision of Korean Association for Public Administration. Seoul: Korean Association for Public Administration.

Kwon, K. D.(1996). An empirical analysis of trends in Korean public research: Focusing on the articles published in the Korean Public Administration Review(1967–1995). *Korean Public Administration Review,* 30: 439–453.

Lee, H.(2001). Applying multidimensional theory into dichotomies of policy analysis: process and policy fact and values. *Korean Policy Studies Review,* 10: 41–42.

Lee, S., & Jung, J.(1996). Analysis of the trends of empirical studies on policy decision making in Korea. *Korean Public Administration Review,* 30: 65–69.

Mo, Changhwan(2007). Korean Policy Analysis: From Economic Efficiency to Public Participation, in Fischer, Frank, et. al., ed.(2007). *Handbook of Public Policy Analysis.* CRC Press.

Part 3. Public Policy Cases

1. Describe the public policy stages(processes).
2. Describe the rational comprehensive model.
3. Describe the garbage can model.
4. Explain the concepts in policy analysis.

Class Exercise

Divide the class into 4 groups.

Each group explains the decision–making processes of the following case based on rational, incremental, satisficing, and garbage can model.

Suppose each group buys a car, describe the decision making process.

Part 4 Public Personnel Administration

Let the public service be a proud and lively career.

—John F. Kennedy, 35th President of the United States

01

Chapter

The Definition of Public Personnel Administration

The highest of distinctions is service to others.

—King George VI

LEARNING OBJECTIVES

After reading Chapter 1, the student should be able to:

1. Understand the meaning of Public Personnel Administration.

Public personnel administration is concerned with how organizations can obtain and retain a work force of effectively performing employees. These we view as the objectives of personnel/human resource management. To achieve them, organizations develop and implement personnel/human resource polices and procedures.

Those policies and procedures, in turn, are shaped by the external environment that the organization confronts and by the ways in which people respond to managerial control systems.

The quality of the organization's work force is critical to the organization's overall success. This observation is especially appropriate in several expanding areas of our economy such as the service sector. The success of governmental organizations, for example, is almost exclusively dependent on their ability to have effective employees.

Public personnel administration can be better explained in terms of the cycles; 1) inputs, 2) conversion process, 3) outputs, and 4) feedback.

Figure 1-1 The Cycle of Public Personnel Administration

Inputs(Legal and politico-social environment)
Merit system, Spoils system, Position classification

⇓

Conversion Process
Recruitment, Selection, Training, Motivation, Performance Appraisal, Compensation

⇓

Outputs
Motivation, Job satisfaction, Organizational Performance,

Feedback
Personnel administration reform

02
Chapter

Inputs of Public Personnel Administration

The miracle is this. The more we share, the more we have.

—Leonard Nimoy, Actor, "Star trek" Series

LEARNING OBJECTIVES

After reading Chapter 2, the student should be able to:

1. Understand the Inputs (Legal and politico-social environment) such as Merit system, Spoils system, Position classification.

1. Merit System vs. Spoils System

Merit system means that the recruitment, appointment, retention and promotion of government employees based on ability, education, experience, and job performance. Most merit systems operate as federal, state, and local civil service systems that emphasize demonstrated fitness as the key personnel factor.

Recruitment and selection of the "best qualified" applicant to fill a vacancy, job tenure, position classification, standardization of pay, and promotion and pay increases based on "performance" evaluations are hallmarks of the system.

On the other hand, a government personnel system based on the principle of rewarding members of the wining political party with jobs in the public service is named after the spoils. The spoils system got its name from the old Roman slogan that "To the victor, belongs the spoils."

The spoils system became entrenched in the American political system after President Andrew Jackson established it after taking office in 1829. For Jackson, the spoil system meant: (1) political selection of federal job holders; and (2) rotation in office.

He believed that the government officials of his day were out of touch with the common people and should be replaced. Moreover, for Jackson, government jobs involved basically simple task that ordinary individuals can handle without special training. Party job holders could also function as campaign workers in subsequent elections.

By 1883, however, sentiment had turned against Jacksonian Democracy and its spoils system, and Congress enacted a major civil service reform act aimed at recruitment and appointment of federal personnel based on merit. Although many top-level positions in the national government are filled by political appointment today, the spoils system as defined by President Jackson have disappeared.

Now look at the differences between political appointees who are appointed politically based on the spoils system and careerists that are selected based upon the merit system.

Table 2–1 The Differences between Political Appointee and Careerist

A	ppointed for shorter teams	C	areer–oriented
P	olor in policy positions	A	ligned with long–team goals of agency
P	artisan	R	esponsible for policy implementation
O	riented toward short–team accomplishment	E	quilibrist
I	gnorant intruders	E	xpertise
N	eed to be sensitive to needs of elected officials, party	R	esponsible to professional work more than to party
T	ransient executives	I	nveterate, permanent
E	go and self–esteem needs	S	ides more with "general public" than with party
E	xecutive or mgt–oriented	T	enets(or doctrines) of good mgt are held in common and shared with most careerists
S	ensitive to own career after public service	S	ensitive to needs of merit system

2. Position Classification

The clustering of government jobs according to their nature, qualifications required, duties performed, and responsibilities assumed. Position classification is used to provide equal pay for equal work for government employees. In the federal civil service, a General Schedule is used to classify jobs according to their nature and the pay involved from GS–1 to GS–15, with the pay at the highest level approximately sevenfold greater than at the lowest level.

The system of the United States government civil service has evolved into a complex set of systems that include principally the General Schedule(GS) for white–collar employees at levels 1 through 15(in Korean case. Grade 9 to 4), Federal Wage System(FWS) for blue–collar employees, Senior Executive System(SES) for Executive–level employees(in Korean case. Grade 3 to 1) and the Executive Schedule for high–ranking federal employees.

Table 2-2 The Pay System for General Schedule(GS)

Pay grade	Lowest step(1)	Highest step(10)
GS-1	$17,803	$22,269
GS-2	$20,017	$25,191
GS-3	$21,840	$28,392
GS-4	$24,518	$31,871
GS-5	$27,531	$35,657
GS-6	$30,577	$39,748
GS-7	$33,979	$44,176
GS-8	$37,631	$48,917
GS-9	$41,563	$54,028
GS-10	$45,771	$59,505
GS-11	$50,287	$65,371
GS-12	$60,274	$78,355
GS-13	$71,674	$93,175
GS-14	$84,697	$110,104
GS-15	$99,628	$129,517

Source: U.S. Office of Personnel Management(2012).

Position classification is an attempt to deal fairly with all employees by establishing standardized categories with extensive job descriptions for each. One of the objectives underlying the system is that maintaining morale among employees by providing for equal treatment.

Position classification also aids in recruitment and hiring by permitting the use of standardized tests to determine qualification. Within each classification, promotion to higher class and merit pay are utilized to encourage excellence in performance.

Position classification also provides for clear lines of authority and responsibility and facilitates the operations of a hierarchical and structured organization. Merit systems utilizing some for of position classification are commonplace today in federal, state, and local personnel administration.

Table 2-3 Employment by Federal Government Agency

	United States	DC area		United States	DC area
Combined Total	1,774	284			
Executive departments	1,593	234	Independent agencies	179	48
Defense, total	623	65	Social Security Administration	62	2
Army	223	19	NASA	18	4
Navy	168	24	Environmental Protection Agency	18	5
Air Force	152	6	Tennessee Valley Authority	12	0
Other defense	80	16	General Services Administration	12	4
Veterans Affairs	239	7	Small Business Administration	6	1
Homeland Security	149	20	Office of Personnel Management	5	2
Treasury	109	14	Other independent agencies	45	30
Justice	105	23			
Agriculture	92	11	Executive departments(cont.)		
Interior	66	7			
Health/Human Services(HHS)	60	28	Energy	15	5
Transportation	53	9	State	14	12
Commerce	39	21	Housing/Urban Dev(HUD)	10	3
Labor	16	6	Education	4	3

Source: U.S. Office of Personnel Management(2012).

03 Chapter

Conversion Process in Personnel Administration

There is no greater calling than to serve your fellow men. There is no greater contribution than to help the weak. There is no greater satisfaction than to have done it well.

—Walter Reuther

LEARNING OBJECTIVES

After reading Chapter 3, the student should be able to:

1. Understand the Conversion Process such as Recruitment, Selection, Training, Motivation, Performance Appraisal, Compensation.

1. Recruitment

Recruitment is the foundation of effective government: The public sector's ability to achieve outcomes, as promised in the law and in budgets, is directly dependent on the quality of its most important and enduring inputs—public servants.

2. Performance Appraisal

By any standard, performance management in the traditional model of administration was inadequate, and this applies to both the performance of individuals and organization. Measures which did exist were ad hoc and far from systematic. It is true that there are difficulties in measuring performance in the public sector when compared to the private sector, but it seemed that little effort was made. Perhaps it was assumed that results would follow from bureaucratic organization, so that any explicit measure was unnecessary.

There was often no idea what was produced, how well it was produced, who was to take the praise or blame, or even who was a good worker. In any case, an administrator does not need to worry about performance as all he or she is doing is carrying out instructions, and performance measurement is the problem of those giving the instructions.

Evaluation of programmes or people was infrequent and inadequate, with no idea of progress towards objectives, if indeed there were any clear objectives.

3. Compensation

The principal problem in the establishment of a compensation plan is the lack of a well-defined wage theory for the public service. Lacking such a theory, those responsible for the preparation of a compensation plan have floundered among various improvised conceptions.

Not by the process of clear formulation but by rationalization from practices that seem prevalent, wage-setting for per-annum employees in the public service appears to be generally based on the minimum rate necessary to obtain qualified employees. In brief, government has not attempted to set a high rate for private industry to emulate but has more usually adopted a rate which is not as low as the lowest-paying rate in industry nor as high as the highest.

04

Chapter

Outputs and Feedback in Public Personnel Administration

LEARNING OBJECTIVES

After reading Chapter 4, the student should be able to:

1. Understand the Outputs such as Motivation, Job satisfaction, Organizational Performance.

Outputs in public personnel administration such as motivation has been already dealt with in Part 2 Organization Theory. Generally speaking, performance measurement systems are the weak link in personnel administration in many countries.

For instance, there may be a lack of explicit standards. Similarly, there may be a reluctance to develop standards for cultural and social reasons. In many cases job responsibilities may be too poorly defined for a meaningful appraisal of performance.

The task of performance appraisal becomes even more difficult at the higher echelons of administration. The difficulties may be due to technical issues, as well as bureaucratic and attitudinal dynamics.

Reforms to public personnel administration are a particularly important part of feedback in public personnel administration. Agencies in many parts of government are now expected to develop performance indicators, that is, some way of measuring the progress the organization and each public servant has made towards achieving declared objectives.

Statistical measures can be developed in any organization, although there are more difficulties in practice in the public sector than usually experienced in the private sector.

References

Cooper, Terry(2006). *The Responsible Administrator.* John Wiley & Sons, Inc.

Geuras, Dean & Carofalo, Charles(2005). Practical Ethics in Public Administration. Management concepts.

Gustafson, J.(1965). Notes on Theology and Ethics, In D. Jenkins (ed.), *The Scoe of Theology.* Cleveland, Ohio: World Publishing.

Jones, W. J., Sontag, F., Becker, M. O., & Fogelin, R.(1969). *Approaches to Ethics.* New York: McGraw−Hill.

Means, R.(1970). *The Ethical Imperative.* New York: Doubleday.

Preston, N.(1996). *Understanding Ethics.* Sydney: Federation Press.

Part 4. Public Personnel Administration Cases

1. Explain the inputs of personnel administration.
2. Explain the conversion process of personnel administration.
3. Explain the outputs and feedback of personnel administration.
4. Compare the merit system and the spoils system.
5. Compare the features of appointees and careerists.

Part 5 Public Budgeting

An institution which is financed by a budget — or which enjoys a monopoly which the customer cannot escape — is rewarded for what it deserves rather than what it earns. It is paid for 'good intentions' and 'programs.' It is paid for not alienating important constituents rather than satisfying any one group. It is misdirected by the way it is being paid into defining performance and results as what will produce the budget rather than as what will produce contribution.

— Peter Drucker

01 Chapter

The Brief History of Budgeting

Waste in Government does not come tied up in neat packages. It is marbled throughout our bureaucracies. It is embedded in the way we do business.

—David Osborne & Ted Gaebler

LEARNING OBJECTIVES

After reading Chapter 1, the student should be able to:

1. Understand the brief history of budgeting.

The recent history of budgeting is filled with numerous failed efforts to put it into practice, as well as with a series of aborted reforms, such as Line-Item Budgeting Systems(LIBS), Planning-Programming Budgeting Systems (PPBS), Zero-Based Budgeting System(ZBBS), and Program Budgeting System (PBS). Many governments use a variety of hybridized versions to address the specific needs of the organization.

Why is it so difficult to operationalize the sensible idea of allocating resources on the basis of the public purposes they serve? What is so difficult about rearranging budget classifications so that they correspond to the basic aims of government?

Part of the answer lies in the multiplicity of governmental purposes. What, for example, is the overriding purpose of money spent on public schools? Is it to educate children, or to prepare them for a livelihood or adulthood, or perhaps to mold them into competent citizens?

Each objective is promoted by public education, but each leads to a different structure of budget accounts. In as much as a government can have only one program structure.

LIBS is a budget in which each expense is separately accounted for, and placed on a separate line for readability and analysis. Line item budgets are useful for financial planning, cost reduction measures, and identifying potential sources of waste or fraud.

The line-item budget approach has several advantages that account for its wide use. It offers simplicity and ease of preparation. It is a familiar approach to those involved in the budget development process. This method budgets by organizational unit and object and is consistent with the lines of authority and responsibility in organizational units. As a result, this approach enhances organizational control and allows the accumulation of expenditure data at each functional level. Finally, line-item budgeting allows the accumulation of expenditure data by organizational unit for use in trend or historical analysis.

PPBS is a concept that stresses the importance of establishing a strong linkage between planning and budgeting. It emanates from the policy of the government to formulate and implement a national budget that is an instrument of national development, implement a national budget that is an instrument of national development, reflective of national objectives, strategies and plans, reflective of national objectives, strategies and plans.

Planning–programming budgeting is an answer to the need for an economic allocation of resources and the undertaking of government policy, program analysis, and cost utility analysis to improve the policy decision process of government. The scheme requires agency managers to identify program objectives, develop measuring program output, calculate total program costs over the long–run, prepare detailed multi–year program and financial plans, and analyze the costs and benefits of alternative program designs.

ZBB(Zero–Based Budgeting) is a method of budgeting in which all expenses must be justified for each new period. Zero–based budgeting starts from a "zero base" and every function within an organization is analyzed for its needs and costs. Budgets are then built around what is needed for the upcoming period, regardless of whether the budget is higher or lower than the previous one.

Because of its detail–oriented nature, zero–based budgeting may be a rolling process done over several years, with only a few functional areas reviewed at a time by managers or group leadership.

PBS(Program Budgeting System) is a simple idea. The basic idea is that budget information and decisions should be structured according to the objectives of the government. It is, however, a time–consuming process that takes much longer than traditional, cost–based budgeting.

In a strict performance budgeting environment, budgeted expenditures are based on a standard cost of inputs multiplied by the number of units of an activity to be provided in that time period. The total budget for an organization is the sum of all the standard unit costs multiplied by the units expected to be provided. And it organizes the budget into quantitative estimates of costs and accomplishments and focuses on measuring and evaluating outcomes.

Table 1–1 Budget System and Primary Function

Acronym	Budget System	Primary Function
LIBS	Line–Item Budget System	Control
PBS	Performance Budgeting System	Management
PPBS	Planning Programming Budget System	Planning
ZBB	Zero Based Budgeting	Cutback

The logic model is a simplified representation of a program or initiative, and illustrates the logical relationship between resources, activities, and expected results.

The logic model may appear as(in case of city library):

The Planned Work might be program. The Inputs are the available or desired resources to undertake the Activities(the number of librarians and library budget).

The Activities are the planned measures or interventions(purchasing and lending books).

The Intended Results might be the program or policy performance.

The Outputs are the results of the Activities(the number of library users).

The Outcomes will be the immediate and intermediate(medium－term) expected results(satisfaction level of library users), and

The Impact will be the long－term or ultimate objective(trust level of library users on the city).

Figure 1－1 Using the Logframe for Program Design in Program Budgeting

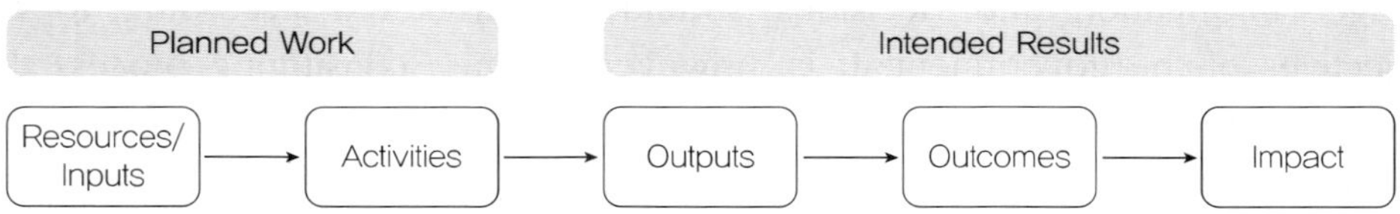

Source: Guiding Program Direction with Logic. W. K. Kellog Foundation.

Korea's fiscal management has evolved in tandem with changes in the social environment and development of the national economy. The 1980s heralded a shift in policy from economic growth to economic stabilization.

The government tightened fiscal policy in response to inflationary pressure and rising aggregate demand. During this period, monetary and fiscal policies were tightened, and the principle of expenditure within revenue or balanced budget principle, was adhered to as more emphasis came to be placed on economic stabilization. Zero－based budgeting was introduced and spending was reprioritized. To support these efforts current and new projects were reviewed in the context of the zero－based budgeting principle by the Budget Review Committee.

02 Chapter The Public Budgeting Process

The more revenue, the more spending.

LEARNING OBJECTIVES

After reading Chapter 2, the student should be able to:

1. Understand the budgeting processes.

Government budgeting is a critical component of public financial management. Budgeting is the process of allocating finite resources to the prioritized needs of an organization. In most cases, for a governmental entity, the budget represents the legal authority to spend money.

The budgeting process includes decision making on all public finance matters, as well as the actual management of government revenues and expenditures. The budget and the process for formulating it reflect both the true intentions of government and how they will be translated into actual programmes and projects.

Many laymen and non-financial administrators think of the budget as an isolated yearly event. The image is reinforced through the annual presentation of the budget to the legislative body by the chief executive. Presentation of the budget is a major milestone in the budget process, and the tax and spending proposals receive great interest from citizens and government operating departments.

The reality of the government budgeting process is that it is part of the administrative process and is continuous throughout the year, entailing many activities and dimensions.

One aspect of the process involves fiscal planning. This is usually conducted by a central agency which provides guidelines to government for the allocation of resources. Even when fiscal planning is weak or non-existent, the central agency has to prepare revenue estimates and some parameters for expenditures in the coming years.

Over time budgeting has come to be governed by a number of principles that are applicable to all countries. These principles remain valid in spirit for different countries, even when subject to modification to meet local needs. The principles include the following:

1. Budget preparation and execution are executive functions;
2. Budget authorization and enforcement of accountability are legislative functions;
3. The budget cycle is periodical, usually on a yearly basis;
4. Budget authorization is specific for objects of expenditure for each major department of government;
5. Budgets are comprehensive and include all government income and expenditures;

6. Budgetary accounts must be uniform for all transactions;
7. A single consolidated fund is the destination of all revenues and the source of all expenditures covered in the budget.

Here's what needs to happen before we officially have a budget for the fiscal year that began more than two months ago:

1. The House and Senate will vote on the top-line discretionary spending numbers negotiated by Murray and Ryan. The House will take up the vote this week and then send the bill over to the Senate.
2. House and Senate appropriators — the lawmakers who allocate money to agencies — will use those top-line numbers to finish work on individual budget bills. In other words, now that the appropriators know how much they can spend, they can hammer out the details.
3. Most likely, the individual budget bills will be combined into a single bill called an omnibus, which will have to pass both chambers.
4. President Obama will sign the omnibus into law, and the U.S. will have a budget for 2014.

Figure 2-1 Federal Budget Process

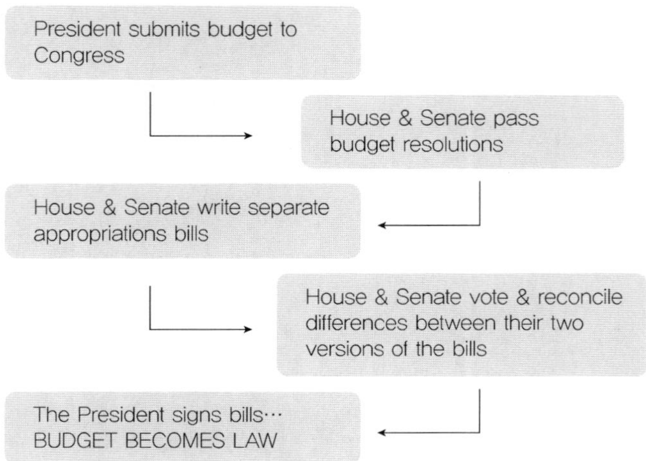

Source: https://www.nationalpriorities.org/blog/2013/12/11/budget-deal-do-we-have-budget-yet-and-then-what/

References

Johnson, Frank(2003). *Financial Accounting for Local and State School Systems.* U.S. Department of Education.

Wildavsky, Aaron B.(1984). *The Politics of the Budgetary Process.* Little, Brown.

http://www.cbpp.org/research/policy-basics-introduction-to-the-federal-budget-process

https://www.nationalpriorities.org/blog/2013/12/11/budget-deal-do-we-have-budget-yet-and-then-what/

Appendix Public Administration Glossary of Terms

The following list of selected terms and concepts are commonly used in public administration.

Source: The On-line Glossary on Governance and Public Administration, made by the Division for Public Administration and Development Management (DPADM) of the United Nations(UN) in collaboration with UN Committee of Experts in Public Administration(CEPA), http://www.unpan.org/Directories/UNPublicAdministrationGlossary/tabid/928/language/en-US/Default.aspx

and Wyatt Hundrup(2000), Maxwell School of Citizenship and Public Affairs.

ACCOUNTABILITY: A political principle according to which agencies or organizations, such as those in government, are subject to some form of external control, causing them to give a general accounting of and for their actions; an essential concept in democratic public administration.

AD HOC: A Latin term meaning temporarily; for this one time. It is sometimes used to criticized methods that substitute for standard procedures.

ADMINISTERED PRICES: Prices determined by other than market forces such as those set by monopolies, cartels, or governments.

ADMINISTRATION: 1. The management and direction of the affairs of governments and institutions. 2. A collective term for all policy making officials of a government. 3. The execution and implementation of public policy. 4. The time in office of a chief executive such as a president, governor, or mayor. 5. The supervision of the estate of a dead person to pay taxes and assign assets to heirs.

ADMINISTRATIVE ACCOUNTABILITY: That aspect of administrative responsibility by which officials are held answerable for general notions of democracy and morality as well as for specific legal mandates.

ADMINISTRATIVE AGENCY: 1. A government organization set up to implement a law. 2. Any civilian government body(board, bureau, department, or individual), other than a court or legislature, that deals with the rights of private parties by adjudication, rule making, investigation, prosecuting, and so on.

ADMINISTRATIVE DECENTRALIZATION: Administrative decentralization seeks to redistribute authority, responsibility and financial resources for providing public services among different levels of government. It is the transfer of responsibility for the planning, financing and management of certain public functions from the central government and its agencies to field units of government agencies, subordinate units or levels of government, semi-autonomous public authorities or corporations, or area-wide, regional or functional authorities. The three major forms of administrative decentralization are deconcentration, delegation, and devolution.

ADMINISTRATIVE DISCRETION: The ability of individual administrators in a bureaucracy to make significant choices affecting management and operation of programs for which they are responsible; particularly evident in separation-of-powers systems.

ADMINISTRATIVE DUE PROCESS: Term encompassing a number of points in administrative law that require that the administrative procedures of government agencies and regulatory commissions, as they affect private parties, be based upon written guidelines that safeguard individual rights and protect against the arbitrary or inequitable exercise of government authority.

ADMINISTRATIVE LAW: 1. That branch of law concerned with the procedures by which administrative agencies make rules and adjudicate cases; the conditions under which these actions can be reviewed by courts. 2. The legislation that creates administrative agencies. 3. The rules and 4 regulations promulgated by administrative agencies. 4. The law governing judicial review of administrative actions.

ADMINISTRATIVE MORALITY: The use of ethical, political, or social precepts to create standards by which the quality of public administration may be judged; such as the standards of honesty, responsiveness, efficiency effectiveness, competence, effect on individual rights, adherence to democratic procedures, and social equity.

ADMINISTRATIVE ORDER: A directive carrying the force of law issued by an administrative agency after adjudication.

ADMINISTRATIVE REFORM: Public administration reforms generally refer to the modernization of government bureaucracy to achieve a better regulation, positively influencing citizen's day-by-day life and businesses. They mainly affect: the way public administrations are structured and respective tasks allocated, the relations among different bodies and the terms and conditions of employment for public servants and public managers (administrative organization); or the way public bodies operate, procedures and principles followed to take decisions, and the way public interests are served and represented (administrative and regulatory procedures).

ADMINISTRATIVE REMEDY: A means of enforcing a right by going to an administrative agency either for help or for a decision. People are often required to exhaust all administrative remedies by submitting their problems to the proper agency before taking their cases to court.

ADMINISTRATOR: 1. A manager. 2. The head of a government agency. 3. Someone appointed by a court to handle a deceased person's estate. 4. Anyone with fiduciary responsibility.

AFFIRMATIVE ACTION PLAN: An organization's written plan to remedy past discriminationagainst, or underutilization of, women and minorities. The plan itself usually consists of a statement of goals, timetables for achieving them, and specific program efforts.

AGENDA SETTING: 1. The process of deciding what issues will be considered at a formal meeting. 2. The process by which ideas or issues come up through the various political processes to wind up on the agenda of a political institution, such as a legislature or court. The process makes extensive use of the mass media to take a relatively unknown or unsupported issue and through publicity expand the numbers who care about the issue, so an institution whether it be city hall or the U.S. Congress, is forced to take some action.

AMENDMENT: 1. A change in a prior law by the enactment of a new law. 2. A change in a bill during its time of consideration in a legislature. 3. A provision of a constitution adopted since its original ratification.

APOLITICAL: 1. Outside of politics; not concerned with political dominance; apathetic toward voting or politics. 2. Nonpartisan; not affiliated with a political party.

APPEAL: 1. Any proceeding or request to a higher authority that a lower authority's decision be reviewed. 2. A formal request to a higher court that it review the actions of a lower court.

APPORTIONMENT: Process by which funds are allocated to agencies for specific portion of the year.

APPROPRIATION: Funds set aside by a legislature to pay for something authorized by law.

AUTHORITY: Power defined according to a legal and institutional framework, and vested in aformal structure (a nation, organization, profession); power exercised through recognized, legitimate channels.

AUTOCRACY: Government by one.

BASE: The point from which most budgetary calculations begin, generally that appropriation which the agency received in the previous fiscal year, with the expectation that spending in each agency will approximate the existing level of expenditures.

BLOCK GRANTS: Grants in which the money can be used for nearly any purpose within a specific function field.

BOUNDARY SPANNING: Representing an organization to outside groups and organizations.

BOUNDED RATIONALITY: Seeking the best possible solution, but not necessarily the most rational from a purely economic standpoint.

BUDGET DEFICIT: When public spending exceeds tax revenues.

BUDGET PADDING: Proposing a higher budget than is actually needed.

BUDGET SURPLUS: When tax revenues exceed public spending.

BUREAUCRACY: A formal organizational arrangement characterized by division of labor, job specialization with no functional overlap, exercise of authority through a vertical hierarchy (chain of command) and a system of internal rules, regulations, and record keeping; the administrative branch of government (national, state, local).

CATEGORICAL OR PROJECT GRANTS: Grants requiring that the money may be spent for only a limited purpose; typically available on a competitive basis.

CHARTER: Local government's equivalent of a constitution.

CIVIL SERVICE: Body of government employees entrusted with the administration of the country, and mandated to carry out the policy of the government of the day.

CITIZEN PARTICIPATION: The involvement of citizens in a wide range of administrative policymaking activities, including the determination of levels of service, budget priorities, and the acceptability of physical construction projects, in order to orient government programs toward community needs, build public support, and encourage a sense of cohesiveness within neighborhoods.

COLLECTIVE BARGAINING: The process by which an agent chosen by public employees negotiates a formal labor agreement or settles day-to-day labor disputes on behalf of the employees in the areas of wages, benefits, working conditions, and administrative policy with parties representing the top politically elected or appointed executives.

COMMON-POOL PROBLEMS: Problems that occur when public stewardship of resources allocates resources inefficiently.

COMMUNITY DEVELOPMENT: An approach to the administration of social and economic development programs in which government officials are dispatched to the field to act as catalysts at the local level, encouraging local residents to form groups, define their own needs, and develop selfhelp projects. The government provides technical and material assistance and helps the community establish institutions, such as farm cooperatives, to carry on the development programs after the officials have left.

COMPARABLE WORTH: Notion that men and women in jobs that are not identical but require similar levels of skill and training should be paid equally.

CONSTITUENCY: Any group or organization interested in the work and actions of a given official, agency, or organization, and a potential source of support for it; also, the interest (sometimes geographic area) served by an elected or appointed public official.

CONTINGENCY APPROACH: The use of different administrative strategies under different conditions; the study of the relationship between factors such as the task an agency performs or the technology it uses and the style of supervision, type of organizational design, and other administrative strategies that will work best given those factors.

COOPERATIVE FEDERALISM: Greater sharing of responsibilities between federal and state governments.

CO-OPTATION: Alliance building between an administrative agency and a clientele group in which the clientele group is allowed to influence agency policy making, in return for which the clientele group tacitly agrees to support the general mission of the agency, provide it with political support, and defend the agency against assaults on its powers, programs, or budget.

CORPORATIONS: Legal entities created by states, which approve charters submitted by founders.

CORRUPTION: Corruption is operationally defined as the misuse of entrusted power for private gain. Transparency International further differentiates between "according to rule" corruption and "against the rule" corruption. Facilitation payments, where a bribe is paid to receive preferential treatment for something that the bribe receiver is required to do by law, constitute the former. The latter, on the other hand, is a bribe paid to obtain services the bribe receiver is prohibited from providing.

COST-BENEFIT ANALYSIS: Technique designed to measure relative gains and losses resulting from alternative policy or program options; emphasizes identification of the most desirable cost benefit ratio, in quantitative or other terms.

COST-BENEFIT RATIO: The proportional relationship between expenditure of a given quantity of resources and the benefits derived therefrom; a guideline for choosing among alternatives, of greatest relevance to the rational model of decision making.

DECISION ANALYSIS: Technique where decisions are likely to be made sequentially and under some degree of uncertainty.

DECISION TREE: Technique that identifies various possible outcomes, given the risks associated with each.

DELEGATION: Assigning tasks to others.

DEMOCRACY: A political system in which decision making power is widely shared among members of the society.

DIALECTICAL ORGANIZATION: A post-bureaucratic form of organization designed to be responsive to clientele needs; dialectical refers to the permanent state of tension between the tendency toward bureaucratization and the tendency toward responsiveness to clients, a tension the organization uses to continually renew itself.

DILLON'S RULE: Municipalities have only those powers granted in their charters; cities are creatures of the state. The opposite of Homerule

DISTRIBUTIVE POLICY: Policy involving use of general tax funds to provide assistance and benefits to individuals or groups.

DIVIDENDS: Payments made to owners of corporations.

DIVISION OF WORK: One of the fundamental principles upon which the science of administration is based; increased specialization in the organization of work in order to narrow the range of tasks for which each person is responsible, which in turn increases the need for administrative planning and coordination and raises the productivity of the organization as a whole.

DUAL FEDERALISM: Pattern in which federal and state governments are struggling for power and influenced with little inter-governmental cooperation.

ECONOMIES OF SCALE: When increased levels of production result in decreased average costs of production.

EFFECTIVENESS: Extent to which a program is achieving or failing to achieve its stated objectives.

EFFICIENCY: Relationship between inputs and outputs.

E-GOVERNMENT: E-government is the application of Information and Communication Technology(ICTs) within Public Administration to optimize its internal and external functions. E-Government refers to the use by government agencies of information technologies (such as Wide Area Networks, the Internet, and mobile computing) that have the ability to transform relations with citizens, businesses, and other arms of government.

ENTITLEMENT GRANTS: Grants that provide assistance to persons who meet certain criteria.

ENTITLEMENT PROGRAMS: Programs that provide a specified set of benefits to those who meet certain eligibility requirements.

EQUAL EMPLOYMENT OPPORTUNITY: Refers to efforts to eliminate employment discrimination on the basis of race, ethnic background, sex, age, or physical handicap; ensures that all persons have an equal chance to compete for employment and promotions based on job qualifications.

EQUALITY: The idea that all persons have an equal claim to life, liberty and the pursuit of happiness.

EQUITY: A criterion for allocating resources on the basis of fairness.

ESTATE TAXES: Taxes imposed on the transfer of wealth after the death of a taxpayer.

ETHICS: Process by which we clarify right and wrong and act on what we take to be right.

EVALUATION: The use of research techniques to measure the past performance of a specific program—in particular, the program's impact on the conditions it seeks to modify—for the purposes of changing the operation of the program so as to improve its effectiveness at achieving its objectives.

EXECUTIVE ORDER: A presidential mandate directed to and governing, with the effect of law, the actions of government officials and agencies.

EXPERT SYSTEMS: Computer programs that mimic the decision making processes of human experts within a particular field.

EXTERNAL COSTS: Those costs imposed by majorities on minorities.

FEDERALISM: A constitutional division of governmental power between a central or national government and regional governmental units (such as states), with each having some independent authority over its citizens.

FISCAL POLICY: Public policy concerned with the impact of government taxation and spending on the economy.

FISCAL YEAR(FY): Government's basic accounting period.

FOREIGN SHARE OF DEBT: That share of the national debt held by foreigners.

FORMAL THEORIES OF ORGANIZATION: Theories stressing formal, structural arrangements within organizations, and "correct" or "scientific" methods to be followed in order to achieve the highest degree of organizational efficiency; examples include Weber's theory of bureaucracy and Taylor's scientific management approach.

FORMULA GRANTS: Grants that employ a specific division rule to indicate how much money any given jurisdiction will receive.

FREE RIDERS: Individuals who let others pay for goods they themselves consume.

FULLY FUNDED PENSION FUND: A pension fund that has the financial resources necessary to meet future retirement benefits.

"GARBAGE CAN" theory of organizational choice: A theory of organizational decision making applicable to organizations where goals are unclear, technologies are imperfectly understood, histories are difficult to interpret, and participants wander in and out; such "organized anarchies" operate under conditions of pervasive ambiguity, with so much uncertainty in the decision making process that traditional theories about coping with uncertainty do not apply.

GENERAL FUND: Fund that handles "unrestricted" funds of government.

GOVERNMENT FAILURE: When a public policy results in an inefficient or inequitable outcome.

GRANTS: Transfers of money (and/or property) from one government to another.

HIERARCHY: A characteristic of formal bureaucratic organizations; a clear vertical "chain of command" in which each unit is subordinate to the one above it and superior to the one below it; one of the most common features of governmental and other bureaucratic organizations.

HOME RULE: Provision allowing cities greater autonomy over local activities.

HUMAN RELATIONS THEORIES OF ORGANIZATION: Theories stressing workers' noneconomic needs and motivations on the job that seek to identify these needs and how to satisfy them; focused on working conditions and social interactions among workers.

INCREMENTALISM: A model of decision making that stresses making decisions through limited successive comparisons, in contrast to the rational model; also focuses on simplifying choices rather than aspiring to complete problem analyses, on "satisfying" rather than "maximizing."

INDEPENDENT AGENCIES: Agencies intentionally created outside the normal cabinet organization.

INTEREST GROUP: A private organization representing a portion (usually small) of the general adult population; it exists in order to pursue particular public policy objectives and seeks to influence government activity so as to achieve its particular objectives.

INTERGOVERNMENTAL COMPETITION: A fiscal structure characterized by many competing governments.

INTERGOVERNMENTAL RELATIONS: All the activities and interactions occurring between oramong governmental units of all types and levels within the American federal system.

INTERJURISDICTIONAL EXTERNALITIES: Arise when governments fail to fully account for costs and benefits imposed on citizens of other governments.

INTERNALIZATION OF COSTS: The allocation of resources by private markets on the basis of full social costs.

INTERORGANIZATIONAL NETWORKS: Patterns of relationships within and among various groups and organizations working in a single policy area.

IRON TRIANGLE: Term given to a coalition of interest groups, agency personnel, and members of Congress created to exert influence on a particular policy issue.

ISSUE NETWORKS: Open and fluid groupings of various political actors (in and out of government) attempting to influence policy.

ITEM VETO: A constitutional power available to more than forty of America's governors, under which they may disapprove some provisions of a bill while approving the others.

JURISDICTION: In bureaucratic politics, the area of programmatic responsibility assigned to an agency by the legislature or chief executive; also, a term used to describe the territory within the boundaries of a government entity (as a local jurisdiction).

LEGISLATIVE INTENT: The purposes and objectives of a legislative body, given concrete form in its enactment (though actual intent may change over time); the bureaucracy is assumed to follow legislative intent in implementing laws.

LEGISLATIVE OVERSIGHT: The process by which a legislative body continually supervises the work of the bureaucracy in order to ensure its conformity with legislative intent.

LIBERAL DEMOCRACY: A fundamental form of political arrangement, founded on the concepts of popular sovereignty and limited government.

LIBERTY: The idea that individual citizens of a democracy should have a high degree of selfdetermination.

LIMITED GOVERNMENT: A central concept of American politics, holding that because government poses a fundamental threat to individual liberties, it must be carefully limited in its capacity to act arbitrarily; the Founders of American government believed it was to be achieved through separation of powers, checks and balances, federalism, and judicial review.

LINE-ITEM BUDGET: Budget format for listing categories of expenditures along with amounts allocated to each.

MANAGEMENT BY OBJECTIVES(MBO): A management technique designed to facilitate goaland priority-setting, development of plans, resource allocation, monitoring progress towards goals, evaluating results, and generating and implementing improvements in performance.

MANDATE: Order requiring a government to do something.

MARKET FAILURE: When the private market fails to produce an efficient or equitable outcome.

MERIT PAY: Increases in salary and wages that are tied to actual quality of work performed.

MERIT PRINCIPLE: Concept that selections of government employees should be based on merit or competence rather than personal or political favoritism.

MERIT SYSTEM: A professional system of personnel administration, free from political interference, in which selection and progress in the service are based upon the performance, expertise, and technical qualifications of each employee, measured objectively, (often through open, competitive examinations), accompanied by the development of a position classification and salary standardization system and administered through offices of personnel administration and a central civil service commission.

MIXED SCANNING: A model of decision making that combines the rational-comprehensive model's emphasis on fundamental choices and long-term consequences with the incrementalists' emphasis on changing only what needs to be changed in the immediate situation.

MODERN ORGANIZATION THEORY: A body of theory emphasizing empirical examination of organizational behavior, interdisciplinary research employing varied approaches, and attempts to arrive at generalizations applicable to many different kinds of organizations.

MONOPOLY GOVERNMENT: A public sector characterized by a single government.

NATIONAL DEBT: The sum of all unpaid public debt.

NEGATIVE EXTERNALITIES: When private markets fail to allocate resources on the basis of full social costs.

NEUTRAL COMPETENCE: The belief that a neutral public bureaucracy following the mandates of a legislative body will meet the requirements of democracy.

NEW PUBLIC ADMINISTRATION: A general movement inspired mainly by younger scholars who challenged several tenets of public administration, primarily the emphasis upon value-neutrality in administrative research and practice, and appealed to scholars and practitioners to take a more proactive role, guided not only by the search for efficiency, but by a sensitivity to the forces of change, the needs of clients, and the problems of social equity in service delivery.

NEW PUBLIC MANAGEMENT: According to Osborne & Gaebler(1993), new public management calls on Government to focus on achieving results rather than primarily conforming to procedures and to adopt market-like competition, innovations and entrepreneurial strategies. In order to be market-like, Government and public administration generally is called upon to be customer-driven and to rely on market-based mechanisms to deliver public services.

NONPROFIT ORGANIZATIONS: Organizations prohibited by law from distributing surplus revenues to individuals.

OFFICE OF MANAGEMENT AND BUDGET(OMB): An important entity in the Executive Office of the U.S. President that assists the president in assembling executive-branch budget requests, coordinating programs, developing executive talent, and supervising program management processes in national government agencies.

OFFICE OF PERSONNEL MANAGEMENT(OPM): A key administrative unit in the national government operating under presidential direction; it is responsible for managing the national government personnel system, consistent with presidential personnel policy.

OLIGARCHY: Government by the few.

OMBUDSMAN: Permanent office that receives complaints and acts on behalf of citizens to secure information, request services, or pursue grievances.

OPEN SYSTEMS THEORY: A theory of organization that views organizations not as simple, "closed" bureaucratic structures separate from their surroundings, but as highly complex, facing considerable uncertainty in their operations, and constantly interacting with their environment; assumes that organizational components will seek an "equilibrium" among the forces pressing on them and their own responses to those forces.

ORGANIZATIONAL CHANGE: A theory of organization that focuses on those characteristics of an organization that promote or hinder change; assumes that demands for change originate in the external environment, and that the organization should be in the best position to respond to them.

ORGANIZATIONAL CULTURE: Basic patterns of attitudes, beliefs, and values that underlie an organization's operation.

ORGANIZATIONAL HUMANISM: A set of organization theories stressing that work holds intrinsic interest for the worker, that workers seek satisfaction in their work, that they want to work rather than avoid it, and that they can be motivated through systems of positive incentives (such as participation in decision making).

ORGANIZATION DEVELOPMENT: A theory of organization that concentrates on increasing the ability of an organization to solve internal problems of organizational behavior as one of its routine functions; concerned primarily with identification and analysis of such problems.

PARTICIPATORY DEMOCRACY: A political and philosophical belief in direct involvement by affected citizens in the processes of governmental decision making; believed by some to be essential to the existence of democratic government; related term is citizen participation.

PERFORMANCE APPRAISAL: Specific evaluation with respect to an individual's progress in completing specified tasks.

PERFORMANCE AUDITING: Analysis and evaluation of the effective performance of agencies in carrying out their objectives.

PERFORMANCE BUDGET: Budget format organized around programs or activities (rather than the objects it purchases), including various performance measurements that indicate the relationship between work actually done and its cost.

PLANNING-PROGRAMMING-BUDGETING SYSTEM(PPBS): Effort to connect planning, systems analysis, and budgeting in a single exercise.

PLURALISM: A social and political concept stressing the appropriateness of group organization, and diversity of groups and their activities, as a means of protecting broad group interests in society; assumes that groups are good and that bargaining and competition among them will benefit the public interest.

POLICY: Statement of goals and intentions with respect to a particular problem or set of problems.

POLICY ANALYSIS: Process of researching or analyzing public problems to provide policy makers with specific information about the range of available policy options and advantages and disadvantages of different approaches.

POLICY IMPLEMENTATION: A general political and governmental process of carrying out programs in order to fulfill specified policy objectives; a responsibility chiefly of administrative agencies, under chief executive and/or legislative guidance; also the activities directed toward putting a policy into effect.

POLITICS/ADMINISTRATION DICHOTOMY: The belief, growing out of the early administrative reform movement and its reaction against the spoils system, which held that political interference in administration would erode the opportunity for administrative efficiency, that the policy making activities of government ought to be wholly separated from the administrative functions, and that administrators had to have an explicit assignment of objectives before they could begin to develop an efficient administrative system.

POLITICS OF THE BUDGETARY PROCESS: The requirement that administrators act as advocates for their own programs during the appropriation process by soliciting outside support, protecting their budgetary base, and inching ahead with new programs; a budgetary system that deals with complex problems by relying upon incremental methods of decision making, information drawn from past experience rather than analysis, and satisfactory rather than optimal standards of quality.

POSITION CLASSIFICATION: Analyzing and organizing jobs on the basis of duties, responsibilities, and the knowledge and skills required to perform them.

PRIVATIZATION: Use of nongovernmental agencies to provide goods and services previously provided by government, also known as "contracting out."

PROGRESSIVE TAX: One that taxes those with higher incomes at a higher rate.

PROPORTIONAL TAX: One that taxes everyone at the same rate.

PUBLIC ADMINISTRATION: The management and administration of public programs.

PUBLIC–CHOICE ECONOMICS: An approach to public administration based on micro–economic theory which views the citizen as a consumer of government goods and services and would attempt to maximize administrative responsiveness to citizen demand by creating a market system for governmental activities in which public agencies would compete to provide citizens with goods and services. This would replace the current system under which administrative agencies in effect act as monopolies under the influence of organized pressure groups which, the public–choice economists argue, are institutionally incapable of representing the demands of individual citizens.

PUBLIC MANAGEMENT: A field of practice and study central to public administration, emphasizing internal operations of public agencies, focuses on managerial concerns related to control and direction, such as planning, organizational maintenance, information systems, personnel management, and performance evaluation.

PUBLIC POLICY: 1. The organizing framework of purposes and rationales for government programs that deal with specified societal problems; 2. the complex of programs enacted and implemented by the government.

RATIONAL MODEL OF DECISION MAKING: Derived from economic theories of how to make the "best" decisions; involves efforts to move toward consciously-held goals in a way that requires the smallest input of scarce resources; assumes the ability to separate ends from means, rank all alternatives, gather all possible data, and objectively weigh alternatives; stresses rationality in the process of reaching decisions.

REDISTRIBUTIVE POLICY: Policy designed to take taxes from certain groups and give them to another group.

REGRESSIVE TAX: One that taxes those with lower incomes at a proportionately higher rate than those with higher incomes.

REGULATION: Government activity designed to monitor and guide private economic competition; specific actions (characterized as economic regulation) have included placing limits on producers' prices and practices, and promoting commerce through grants or subsidies; other actions emerging more recently (termed social regulation) have included regulating conditions under which goods and services are produced and attempting to minimize product hazards and risks to consumers.

REGULATORY COMMISSION: Group formed to regulate a particular area of the economy: usually headed by a group of individuals appointed by the President and confirmed by the Senate.

REGULATORY POLICY: Policy designed to limit actions of persons or groups to protect all or parts of the general public.

REINVENTING GOVERNMENT: 1. The title of a book written by David Osborne and Ted Gaebler in 1992. 2. Term referring to ideas used in government that are entrepreneurial in nature whose purpose is to improve government services.

REVENUE SHARING: Grant pattern in which the money can be used in any way the recipient government chooses.

RULE MAKING: Administrative establishment of general guidelines for application to a class of people or a class of actions at some future time.

SATISFICING: The process of decision making that characterizes most governmental action; a limited search through familiar patterns of behavior for a course of action that meets pre-established, minimum standards of performance, rather than an exhaustive review of all alternatives in search of the optimal solution to a particular problem.

SCIENTIFIC MANAGEMENT: A formal theory of organization developed by Frederick Taylor in the early 1900s; concerned with achieving efficiency in production, rational work procedures, maximum productivity, and profit; focused on management's responsibilities and on "scientifically" developed work procedures, based on "time and motion" studies.

SENIOR EXECUTIVE SERVICE(SES): Established in the national Civil Service Reform Act of 1978; designed to foster professional growth, mobility, and versatility among senior career officials (and some "political" appointees); incorporated into national government personnel management broad emphasis on performance appraisal and merit pay concepts, as part of both the SES itself and broader merit system reform.

SPECIAL DISTRICTS: Local governments created for a specific purpose within a specific area.

SPAN OF CONTROL: One of the early principles of administration which states that there is an upper limit to the number of subordinates any administrator can directly supervise, generally set at twelve, and advises administrators to eliminate any violations of this principle by reducing the number of officials reporting to them by either merging certain offices or stretching out the hierarchy.

SPOILS SYSTEM: A system of hiring personnel based on political loyalty and connections; can also extend to government contracts and the like; usually takes the form of rewarding party supporters with government jobs.

STAKEHOLDERS: The many different persons or interest groups that are involved in a policy decision and are affected by the results.

STRATEGIC PLANNING: Matching organizational objectives and capabilities to the anticipated demands of the environment to produce a plan of action that will ensure achievement of objectives.

SUBGOVERNMENTS: The tendency of bureaucrats to seek political support for their programs by building informal alliances outside of the official hierarchy with groups that possess resources the bureaucrats lack, primarily with legislative committees and organized interest or pressure groups (also known as iron triangles).

SUNSET LAW: Provision that sets a specific termination date for a program.

SUNSHINE LAW: Provision that requires agencies to conduct business in public view.

SYSTEM: Set of regularized interactions configured or "bounded" in a way that differentiates and separates them from other actions that constitute the system's environment.

SYSTEMS THEORY: A theory of social organizations, holding that organizations — like other organisms — may behave according to inputs from their environment, outputs resulting from organizational activity, and feedback leading to further inputs; also, change in any one part of a group or organizational system that affects all other parts.

TASK FORCES: Groups brought together to work on specific organizational problems. THEORY X and THEORY Y: Two opposing assumptions about people at work that lead to opposing styles of management. Theory X assumes that most people hate work, avoid responsibility, prefer to be directed, and have to be controlled and coerced to put out a fair day's work; Theory Y assumes that people will seek responsibility, demonstrate a high degree of imagination, and exercise self-direction if they have a creative, challenging job to which they can become committed.

TRANSPARENCY: Transparency refers to unfettered access by the public to timely and reliable information on decisions and performance in the public sector, as well as on governmental political and economic activities, procedures and decisions

WELFARE STATE: Political system based on the premise that the government has the responsibility for the well being of its citizens, by ensuring that a minimum standard of living is within everyone's reach. This commitment is translated into provision of universal and free education, universal medical care, insurance against disability, sickness, and unemployment, family allowances for income supplement, and old age pensions.

WHISTLE-BLOWING: Making any disclosure of legal violations (especially within public organizations), mismanagement, a gross waste of funds, an abuse of authority, or a danger to public health or safety, whether the disclosure is made within or outside the formal chain of command.

ZERO-BASE BUDGETING: Budget format that presents information about the efficiency and effectiveness of existing programs and highlights possibilities for eliminating or reducing programs by assuming that the minimum funding level for the agency is zero, thereby requiring agency administrators to justify all expenditures by the same standard of review that normally are applied only to new programs or increments above the base.

INDEX

A

Accountability 84
Adams Equity Theory 138
Adhocracy 149, 152
Administrative Management 129
Agenda Formation 168, 176
Alderfer 137, 138
American Public Administration 18
A New Interpretation of Organizations 121
AUTHORITY 39

B

Basic Perspective on Motivation 136
Behavioral Approach 97
Behavioral Theories 140
Belonginess 137
Big Government 19
Budgeting 203
Budgeting Process 207
Budget System and Primary Function 205
Bureaucracy 37, 129

C

CENTRALIZATION 40
chaos 154
Chaos Theory 152
Class Exercise 161
Classical Organization Theory 130, 157
Closed System Theory 130
Communication Network 117
Comparative Public Administration(CPA) 52
Compensation 188, 195
Concepts in Policy Analysis 176
Concepts in Public Policy 175
concern for people 140
concern for production 140
considerate 140
content theories 138
contingency theory 129
Cost-benefit analysis 176
C-P-N-D(Contents-Platform-Network-Device) ecological system 96

D

Darwinian Selection 131, 147
Decision－Making Support Systems 64
Decision－making Theory 131
Definition of Public Policy 166
Departmentation 43
Descriptive 131
Development Administration(DA) 52
Dichotomy 26
dichotomy between politics and administration 31
DIKW Pyramid 62
Direction 131
dissatisfaction 138
Dissipative Structure 131, 154
Divisionalized Form 149, 151
Division of labour 131
DIVISION OF WORK 39

E

Ecological Approach 93
Economic Incentive 131
Effectiveness 85
employee－centered 140
Employment by Federal Government Agency 193
Entropy 93
Environmental Change 131
Equifinality 93
ERG(Existence, Relatedness, and Growth) 137
ERG theory 137
ESPIRIT DE CORPS(Team Spirit) 41
Esteem 137, 138
Existence 138
expectancy theory 139
Externalities 101

F

Federal Budget Process 209
Feedback 92
Fiedler's Contingency Model 142
fluctuation 154

G

Garbage Can Model 172, 173
Governance 82
Government 82
Government failures 99
Government Information Systems 61
government policy 12
Group Communication Networks 118
Growth 138

H

Hamiltonian Classicism 19
Hersey－Blanchard Situational Leadership 144
Herzberg 138
Hierarchy of authority 131
Homeostasis 93
Human Relations 129, 131
Human Resource Theory 157
Hygiene 138

I

Implementation 176
Incremental Model 171
Informal Group 131
initiating structure 140
innovation and evolution of a system 154

Inputs 92
instability 154
Integration of Motivation Theories 137
Iron Triangle 30

J

Jeffersonian Romanticism 19
Job satisfaction 188

K

Key Parts of an Organization 149
Korean Public Policy 178

L

Lamarckian Adaptation 131, 147
Leader member relations 142
Leadership 139
Levels of Governance 83
Line－Item Budgeting Systems(LIBS) 204
Logframe 206
Long－term 176

M

Machine Bureaucracy 149, 150
Madisonian Neoclassicism 20
Management Information Systems 63
Management Principles 39
Management science 59
Market failures 100
Maslow 138
Merit System 188, 190
middle line 148
Mintzberg's Five Organizational Structures 149
Modern Structural Organization Theory 157
Moral 131
Motivation 131, 136, 138, 188
Motivational Force(MF) 139

N

Necessity of Organizations 117
Need Hierarchy Theory of Maslow 136
Neo－classical Organization Theory 130, 157
New Dichotomy 51
New Public Administration 70
New Public Management 70
Noneconomic Incentive 131

O

Office of the President 45
Ohio State 140
Open System Theory 146
operative core 148
Order out of Chaos 131
Organization as a Culture 126
Organization as a Information－processing Brain 124
Organization as a Machine 122
Organization as a Means to Domination and Exploitation 126
organizational Behavior 129
Organizational change 154
Organizational Performance 188
Organization as an Evolving Organism 123
Organization as a Psychic Prison 125
Organization Theory Cases 159
Organization theory(OT) 129
Outcomes 176
Outputs 176

P

Participation 84
Pay System for General Schedule(GS) 192
Performance Appraisal 188, 195
Personnel administration reform 188
PESTLE Analysis 94
Physiological 137, 138
Planning－Programming Budgeting Systems (PPBS) 204
Policy Adoption 168, 176
Policy evaluation 168, 176
Policy Evaluation and Termination 174
Policy Implementation 168, 174
Policy－making 176
Political Appointee and Careerist 191
Politics/Adm. 26, 51
Population ecology theory 147
POSDCoRB 38
Position Classification 188, 191
Position power 142
Prescriptive 131
Prismatic Model 95
Process of Public Policy 166
Process Theories of Motivation 138
production－centered 140
Professional Bureaucracy 149, 151
Program Budgeting System(PBS) 204
Public Administration 11, 12
Public Choice Theory 98
Public Goods 103
Public Personnel Administration 187, 188
Public Policy 163

Q

Quantitative Management 129

R

Rational－comprehensive Model 170
Receptor 92
Recruitment 188, 195
Redundancy 131
Reinventing Government 70
Relatedness 138
Relay Assembly Room Experiments 41
REMUNERATION(Rewards) 40
Requisite Variety 131
Responsiveness 85
Rule of Law 86

S

Safety 137, 138
satisfaction 138
SCALAR CHAIN 40
Scientific Management 37, 129
security 137
Selection 188
Self－Actualization 137, 138
Self－Organization 131, 152
Self－Organizing 131
Self－Organizing Systems(SOS) 156
Separation of Powers 20
Short－term Outcomes 176
Simon's Bounded Rationality and Satisficing Model 172
Simple Structure 149
Small Government 19
Social 138
Social Network Theory 117
Specialization 131
Spoils System 188, 190
Stages of Policy－making Processes 168

strategic apex 148
Structural Contingency Theory 146
Structure 131
support staff 148
Systematic Management 129
Systems Theory 91, 129, 147, 157

T

technostructure 148
The Executive Branch 46
The Managerial Grid 140
Theory X 134
Theory Y 134
The Proverbs of Administration 54
The task structure 142
Traditional Definition of Organizations 121
Tragedy of the Commons 105
Training 188
Trait Theory 139
Transparency 85
two－factor theory 138
Typology of Organization Theory 131

U

UNITY OF COMMAND 40
University of Michigan 140

V

Vertical Command 131

W

Wilson's Efficient Government in Action 20

Z

ZBB(Zero－Based Budgeting) 205
Zero－Based Budgeting System(ZBBS) 204

저자소개

최창현(Choi, ChangHyeon)

뉴욕주립대 행정 및 정책학 박사, 현 가톨릭관동대 행정학과 교수
한국조직학회 회장 역임
뉴욕주립대 록펠러 행정대학원 객원교수
RPI 테크노 경영대학원 초빙교수
파고다 외국어학원 TOEIC 강사 역임

Introducing Public Administration
Made Simple for TOEIC

펴낸날 제1판 제1쇄 2016년 11월 25일
지은이 최창현
펴낸이 임춘환
펴낸곳 도서출판 대영문화사
주소 서울특별시 용산구 청파로 61길 5(청파동 1가) 제일빌딩 2층
등록 1975년 12월 26일 제3-16호
전화 (02)716-3883, (02)714-3062
팩스 (02)703-3839
홈페이지 http://www.dymbook.co.kr

ISBN 978-89-7644-574-2
값 15,000원